The Effects of Litigation on Health Care Costs

Brookings Dialogues on Public Policy

*The presentations and discussions at Brookings conferences and seminars
often deserve wide circulation as contributions to public understanding
of issues of national importance. The Brookings Dialogues on Public
Policy series is intended to make such statements and commentary
available to a broad and general audience, usually in summary form.
The series supplements the Institution's research publications by
reflecting the contrasting, often lively, and sometimes conflicting views of
elected and appointed government officials, other leaders in public and
private life, and scholars. In keeping with their origin and purpose, the
Dialogues are not subjected to the formal review procedures established
for the Institution's research publications. Brookings publishes them
in the belief that they are worthy of public consideration but does
not assume responsibility for their accuracy or objectivity. And, as
in all Brookings publications, the judgments, conclusions, and
recommendations presented in the Dialogues should not be ascribed to the
trustees, officers, or other staff members of the Brookings Institution.*

The Effects of Litigation on Health Care Costs

Papers by ANN T. HUNSAKER

DEBORAH J. CHOLLET

PATRICIA M. DANZON

JOHN E. PORTER

WENDY K. MARINER

JOHN PRATHER BROWN

presented at a conference at the Brookings Institution,

April 18, 1984

Edited by MARY ANN BAILY and WARREN I. CIKINS

THE BROOKINGS INSTITUTION

Washington, D.C.

Copyright © 1985 by
THE BROOKINGS INSTITUTION
1775 Massachusetts Ave., N.W.
Washington, D.C. 20036

Library of Congress Catalog Card Number 85-70875
ISBN 0-8157-0757-6

9 8 7 6 5 4 3 2 1

About Brookings

THE BROOKINGS INSTITUTION is a private nonprofit organization devoted to research, education, and publication in economics, government, foreign policy, and the social sciences generally. Its principal purpose is to bring knowledge to bear on the current and emerging public policy problems facing the American people. In its research, Brookings functions as an independent analyst and critic, committed to publishing its findings for the information of the public. In its conferences and other activities, it serves as a bridge between scholarship and public policy, bringing new knowledge to the attention of decisionmakers and affording scholars a better insight into policy issues. Its activities are carried out through three research programs (Economic Studies, Governmental Studies, Foreign Policy Studies), a Center for Public Policy Education, a Publications Program, and a Social Science Computation Center.

The Institution was incorporated in 1927 to merge the Institute for Government Research, founded in 1916 as the first private organization devoted to public policy issues at the national level; the Institute of Economics, established in 1922 to study economic problems; and the Robert Brookings Graduate School of Economics and Government, organized in 1924 as a pioneering experiment in training for public service. The consolidated institution was named in honor of Robert Somers Brookings (1850–1932), a St. Louis businessman whose leadership shaped the earlier organizations.

Brookings is financed largely by endowment and by the support of philanthropic foundations, corporations, and private individuals. Its funds are devoted to carrying out its own research and educational activities. It also undertakes some unclassified government contract studies, reserving the right to publish its findings.

A Board of Trustees is responsible for general supervision of the Institution, approval of fields of investigation, and safeguarding the independence of the Institution's work. The President is the chief administrative officer, responsible for formulating and coordinating policies, recommending projects, approving publications, and selecting the staff.

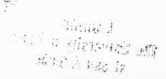

Editors' Preface

THIS LATEST VOLUME in the Brookings Dialogues on Public Policy series is the product of a conference entitled The Effects of Litigation on Health Care Costs. Experts in health care litigation and members of the health care and legal communities considered the effects of the legal system on the changing health care industry. Participants moved from a broad discussion of the issue of liability and health care to specific questions concerning malpractice, the manufacture of drugs and vaccines, public policy, and proposed alternatives to the current system.

The following advisory group members especially contributed to an investigation of the topic: John Prather Brown, Warren I. Cikins, Deborah J. Chollet, Jacqueline Mazza, Joseph N. Onek, John Post, and Raymond Scalettar. Clifford Stromberg also provided helpful insights.

Louise Russell and Henry Aaron, of Brookings, offered valuable advice on structuring the conference, which was held on April 18, 1984, and Donna Marsh provided technical assistance. Theresa B. Walker edited the manuscript, and Chisolm B. Hamilton prepared it for typesetting.

The Brookings Institution is grateful to Merrell Dow Pharmaceuticals, Inc., the Henry J. Kaiser Family Foundation, and the Employee Benefit Research Institute for financial support.

Mary Ann Baily
Warren I. Cikins
Editors

May 1985
Washington, D.C.

Contents

Introduction

MARY ANN BAILY

TURNING to the courts to resolve conflicts and redress grievances has always been a favorite American tactic. But in recent years the American public has become concerned about the growing volume of litigation, particularly health care litigation. Millions of dollars are at stake as more and more often patients sue providers and providers sue regulatory authorities.

At the same time, the cost of health care is increasing greatly. The share of health expenditure in gross national product (GNP) has passed the 10 percent mark, and a national sense is developing that unless drastic steps are taken, expenditures will increase without limit.

Although litigation and rising health care costs have each attracted much attention, less attention has focused on the relationship between the two. Yet clearly a connection exists. First, litigation is expensive, and much of the legal expense becomes a cost to the health care sector. Malpractice insurance premiums are now between 2 percent and 5 percent of expenditures on health care; from 60 percent to 82 percent of that amount goes for legal and administrative costs, rather than patient compensation. The prices of drugs and vaccines incorporate the costs to manufacturers of suits brought by the victims of side effects. The government health budget includes the wages of lawyers who handle litigation concerning government health programs.

Second, the fear of litigation may change behavior in ways that raise costs. Doctors may practice "defensive medicine," ordering tests and procedures to protect themselves against suits rather than to benefit the patient. Manufacturers may incur extra production costs in pursuit of excessive levels of safety, or they may fail to develop a product that reduces health care costs if adverse effects are possible. For example, drugs and vaccines often replace more expensive medical care, but the potential liability for a rare side effect makes them unattractive to a risk-averse manufacturer.

Third, litigation may make it difficult to change the behavior of providers and consumers in ways that lower costs. For example,

1

the fear that patients will sue may make doctors and hospitals reluctant to eliminate care of little benefit relative to cost. Providers and patients may sue third party payers who have constrained choices in the name of cost control by, for example, changing the terms of coverage, imposing cost-effective standards of care, requiring patients to see providers who practice a low-cost style of medicine, or introducing new organizational forms of care delivery.

Of course, even from the narrow perspective of cost control, litigation is not all bad. Injuries caused by malpractice may require expensive medical care to correct them; if the prospect of litigation induces greater carefulness, some of that expense is avoided. And antitrust litigation can foster desirable competition, preventing inefficiency and monopolistic practices.

The possiblity of recourse to the courts also acts as a vital check on the improper use of power, whether by providers, insurers, or government. The peculiarly vulnerable position of patients in the health care system—the importance of health care to their well-being and the trust that patients place in those who care for them—must not be forgotten.

The balance between health care costs and benefits is complicated. In seeking to achieve balance, the effect of the legal system on health care costs, either beneficial or detrimental, must be considered. The Brookings Institution brought together experts in health care litigation as well as members of the health care and legal communities for a one-day forum. Participants explored the topic in general terms and then focused on two prominent types of health litigation: the liability of medical providers for injuries caused by their negligence, that is, malpractice; and the liability of manufacturers of drugs and vaccines for adverse effects caused by the use of their products, that is, product liability.

This volume contains the six major presentations made at the forum. The overview briefly summarizes each of the six presentations; outlines the major points made by the other panelists in response; and gives highlights of the panel's discussion with the audience.

Overview

Three perspectives could be distinguished—those of the policymaker, the economist, and the ethicist. Ann T. Hunsaker, assistant general counsel for the Health Care Financing Administration, opened the forum with a discussion of the federal government's experience, one of obvious importance, since the federal government underwrites nearly a third of personal health expenditure.

The complexity of health legislation fosters litigation. More important, fundamental differences occur in our society over what constitutes proper health policy. When interested groups find a policy decision unacceptable, they often use litigation as an indirect way to challenge it or at least delay its implementation. Ms. Hunsaker's paper cites two examples: litigation over whether the cost of charity care provided by hospitals in exchange for government construction funds is an allowable cost for reimbursement under medicare; and litigation over the proper share of medicare in hospital malpractice insurance premiums. In both cases, the disagreement was not over the interpretation of a statute but over fundamental questions of policy.

Such litigation and the attendant delays in implementation are costly. Further costs are incurred when new policies must be carefully drafted to anticipate legal challenge. Yet, Ms. Hunsaker maintains that disputes over the nature of policy should be settled in the political arena, not in the courts. She approves of the recent trend for Congress and the Department of Health and Human Services to find ways to limit the number of disputes that reach the courts. In setting such limits, she emphasizes the importance of questions of jurisdiction and the proper scope of administrative and judicial review of government actions.

Deborah J. Chollet, of the Employee Benefit Research Institute, surveys the economic literature on the effects of legal liability rules on the allocation of resources. Tort liability relies on two alternative standards: *negligence* and *strict liability*. Under a negligence rule, liability for injury hinges on the failure of the provider of the good or service to take reasonable precautions to protect the consumer. Under strict liability, the provider may be liable even when all reasonable precautions have been taken.

From an economist's perspective, these standards have two goals: *equity* and *efficiency*. Efficiency requires incentives to encourage the allocation of an optimal amount of resources to accident avoidance. Equity requires a fair system of compensation for the economic losses of those injured through no fault of their own. Ms. Chollet examines the nature of liability rules in health care and their effects on equity and efficiency, especially their impact on total health care expenditures. She then considers direct regulation as an alternative to legal liability, arguing that the task is to determine the best mix of the two.

The discussion following these presentations focused on society's expectations from its health care and legal systems. What are these expectations? Who creates them? How have they been changing over time? Panelist Mary Ann Baily, a health economist at George Washington University, noted that the law plays a role as the expression of society's collective conscience. Litigation in which ethical principles are at issue is common and has significant implications for health care costs. The termination of life-sustaining treatment, the duty of a hospital or doctor to treat those who cannot afford to pay, and the propriety of limiting care when the benefits are not worth the cost (rationing) exemplify cases distinguished by unresolved ethical questions. Is it ever acceptable to allow a patient to die, and if so, under what circumstances? Is society obligated to provide care to the poor, and if so, how much care must they receive and who should pay? Is it ethical for doctors to consider the cost of care when making clinical decisions? Because there is no societal consensus on these questions, these cases are ending up in court.

Willis Goldbeck, of the Washington Business Group on Health, expanded on the economic perspective. He emphasized the current major restructuring of the health care industry, which will produce economic losers as well as winners (and in our society, losers often resort to the courts). He then discussed the rising cost of health care as experienced by large employers and unions. They pay ever-increasing sums for employee health insurance coverage and are questioning whether these huge sums produce benefits worth the cost. They see the high cost of malpractice litigation as one place where savings could occur, for example, by moving from the tort system to arbitration. They are also searching for ways to encourage efficiency in health care provision and for better information about prices and outcomes to use in making appropriate tradeoffs between quality and cost. They view antitrust litigation as a potential instrument in the pursuit of these goals.

Malpractice and health

Patricia Danzon, professor of economics at Duke University, opened the session on malpractice with the observation that the system of malpractice litigation and other mechanisms to deter malpractice are costly, but the cost is often exaggerated. Moreover, the cost of malpractice itself is much greater than the cost of litigation. It is difficult to measure the extent to which the system of malpractice litigation deters injuries; however, her rough calculations indicate that the deterrence effect may be sufficient to justify the cost. In her opinion, injury prevention is the primary standard on which the system should be judged, since if compensation is the only object, it can be done more cheaply and equitably by other means.

Although the system of malpractice litigation plays a useful role, certain reforms would make it more cost effective such as a uniform schedule of payments instead of individualized tort liability; shorter statutes of limitations; a standard of care redefined to allow cost as a defense for not taking precautionary measures; and freedom to contract out of tort rights. In setting the schedule of payments, awards for pain and suffering should be modest and limited to permanent injury cases. Compensation under liability rules is a form of social insurance, and compensation for both monetary and nonmonetary loss provides more insurance than the public is willing to pay for.

The other panelists agreed with Professor Danzon that reforms in the legal system to deter malpractice are needed but differed about how urgent the problem is. Those with backgrounds in the provision of health services, Dr. Raymond Scalettar, of the American Medical Association, and William Robinson, of the American Hospital Association, believe that Professor Danzon greatly underestimates the seriousness of the legal system's effect on health care costs. Those with backgrounds in law and consumer advocacy, Joseph Onek, of the law firm of Onek, Klein and Farr, and David Greenberg, of the Consumer Federation of America, concurred with Professor Danzon's assessment.

The session also focused on the advantages and disadvantages of the proposed reforms. In discussing limits on liability, Professor Danzon emphasized the current unpredictability of awards. She argued that smaller but more predictable awards could have the same deterrence value and would be more equitable. Mr. Greenberg countered that limiting liability would not work well and would generate strong opposition from the public. Panel and audience debated the ability of patients to make informed, rational decisions to contract out of tort liability; the difficulty of setting standards of medical practice that take cost into account; and the need for the medical profession to assume a more active role in developing such standards. Participants also discussed the part played by the plaintiff's lawyers and the contingency fee in setting the style of litigation; the advantages and disadvantages of arbitration systems; and the tendency for high malpractice premiums to discourage entry of young doctors into some specialties.

Mr. Onek stressed the changes in the delivery system that are in progress. In a more competitive and cost-conscious health care system, the malpractice system will play a somewhat different and perhaps more important role. Doctors may, for example, use it as a weapon against a cost-cutting hospital administration by arguing that proposed changes will expose the hospital to mal-practice suits.

The experience of other countries was also noted. Malpractice litigation is much less common elsewhere in the world, but the U.S. experience does not exactly parallel that of other countries because of significant differences in history and environment.

Congressional perspectives

Congressman John Porter presented a history of government involvement in the malpractice liability issue at the federal and state levels. He, like Ms. Hunsaker, emphasizes the role of government in the market for health care and the concern for cost that naturally arises. Major alternative approaches to the mal-practice question under consideration by members of Congress range from no action, to encouraging action at the state level, to a federally sponsored no-fault compensation system. The most likely congressional approach is a no-fault model that could be imposed on the states under federal guidelines, such as the Moore-Gephardt Alternative Medical Liability Act recently introduced in Congress.

Congressman Doug Walgren, in his remarks, concurred with Congressman John Porter on the importance of the issue, but he expressed concern over the danger of too much government regulation.

Drugs and vaccines

With Wendy Mariner's paper, the focus shifts from malpractice to product liability. Professor Mariner, assistant professor of health law at the Harvard School of Public Health, explores how litigation may affect the cost of health care through its effects on the development and distribution of drugs and vaccines. In an overview of legal theories of tort liability for personal injury as they apply to these products, she discusses the division of re-sponsibility for adverse effects between manufacturer and physi-cian. An important difference exists between liability for vaccine side effects and that for drug side effects; manufacturers are held to have a duty to warn consumers directly about the adverse effects of vaccines, whereas for prescription drugs, the manufac-turers need only inform physicians.

Professor Mariner reviews the costs that tort law imposes on the manufacturer, the claimant (or his or her lawyer, given con-tingency fee arrangements), and society. Little is known about the size of these costs, although some rough guesses can be made from studies of the costs linked with other tort cases, such as asbestos and automobile injury cases.

Finally, she discusses alternatives to the system of malpractice litigation, distinguishing between the policy problems raised by vaccines and those raised by drugs. In her opinion, the pursuit of excessive levels of safety in response to the tort system ("defensive manufacturing" by analogy to defensive medicine) is not a policy problem for drugs, since in practice, regulation by the Food and Drug Administration (FDA) is the binding constraint. However, for vaccines, a special disincentive is created because manufacturers have an additional duty to warn yet cannot do so directly because they do not control vaccine administration. Moreover, vaccination benefits society, not just the individual. In fact, the law requires some individuals to be vaccinated, so they cannot be said to bear the risks voluntarily. Thus perhaps an approach to liability and compensation for vaccine injuries should differ from one used for drug injuries.

In his remarks, Edward Burger, of Georgetown University Medical Center's Institute for Health Policy Analysis, emphasized the seriousness of the effects of product liability litigation. He noted that between 1968 and 1980, the number of licensed vaccine manufacturers in the United States decreased from thirty-seven to eighteen, of which only eight are producing vaccines at present. Moreover, some vaccines known to be feasible have never been developed for use. Unlike Professor Mariner, he believed that the threat of litigation has significant effects on drug manufacture as well as on vaccine development. It is especially important for three types of drugs: those for chronic illness taken over a long period of time, such as antidiabetic drugs; those used by well persons, such as oral contraceptives; and those intended for serious illnesses, but which have severe side effects, such as anticancer drugs. Joseph Page, professor of law at Georgetown University, agreed, pointing out that FDA penalties can be rather light compared with the compensation that results from litigation; thus the threat of litigation may be the greater deterrent.

Mr. Burger also suggested that it might be valuable to look at experience in Canada, which spends only 10 percent of what the United States spends on this type of litigation, even though the two countries are similar in many ways.

Mr. Page then returned to the theme raised in the first session, law as an expression of ethical values, pointing out that besides compensating and deterring, the tort system punishes. This effect should be considered when thinking about reform. Finally, he said that in assessing the cost of litigation, more information about product liability insurance is needed. What does it cost? Who has it? What role does it play?

Panelists also discussed the swine flu indemnification of vaccine manufacturers and the Hawkins bill for a national vaccine injury compensation program as possible models for reform. The panelists agreed that both the swine flu program and the Hawkins bill were flawed but had potentially useful elements.

The session closed with a discussion of the future. Some think that dramatic technical breakthroughs are on the horizon, which will encourage the development of vaccines for everything from tooth decay to types of cancer. If this is true, the product liability issue may decline in importance as vaccine production becomes attractive enough to manufacturers to compensate for the product liability risk.

Alternatives to the present system

The final session focused specifically on system reform. John Prather Brown, of Chase, Brown and Blaxall, lists the central issues that must be addressed by any reform. These issues are the effect of reform on incentives to take precautions; the cost of operating the system; and the scope of proposed changes (narrow scope means boundaries must be drawn, and boundaries generate litigation). Proposed reforms could also affect funding sources and the system's interaction with other sources of compensation; the respective roles of courts, agencies, and markets in compensation; the predictability of the potential award; and the role of alternate mechanisms, such as mediation and arbitration, for resolving disputes. He notes that the legal system is only one source of incentives to take precautions; others arise directly from consumers' choices and indirect market effects on the firm's reputation. The paper then examines four possibilities for system reform in light of these issues: a quasi-no-fault plan, such as the O'Connell-Moore proposal for malpractice reform; the Federal Uniform Product Liability Law introduced by Senator Robert Kasten; marketability of claims; and a comprehensive no-fault compensation plan for all accidents, modeled on the New Zealand scheme.

Panelists Hans Weill, of Brookings, and Peter Szanton, of Endispute, Inc., discussed litigation over occupational lung disease as an example of health litigation. Dr. Weill said that three distinct medico-legal issues arise in these cases: diagnosis, causation, and impairment. What is the claimant's medical problem? Was it caused by some action of the defendant? To what extent will it cause lifetime disability? These are difficult scientific questions. In particular, causation, which is of the utmost importance in tort cases, can usually be handled only in terms of probabilities. The legal system has not developed a method for deciding this type of case in a consistent, equitable fashion. Dr. Weill advocated a scientifically based set of guidelines, updated as the scientific data base evolves, and an apparatus for objective determinations in individual cases based firmly on these guidelines.

Mr. Szanton said that besides the medical complexity in occupational lung disease cases, problems are caused by variations in the law across states and by the absence of records about insurance coverage, given the long time span between exposure and manifestation of disease. Despite this, in asbestos cases, efforts are being made by various groups of manufacturers, insurers, and leading plaintiffs' lawyers to develop a coordinated private system for resolving claims. Dr. Weill and Mr. Szanton both emphasized the potential for the development of private, nonadversarial systems as alternatives to government-initiated approaches.

There was then a general discussion of alternative mechanisms for resolving disputes (other than the courts or arbitration). These were held to be simpler and to be less likely to end up simply "splitting the difference," as is so often the outcome of traditional arbitration. Alternatives also allow more flexibility in the timing of the development and presentation of facts and in the choice of a third party to resolve the dispute.

Finally, the forum closed with a return to a discussion of the underlying goals of the legal system as it affects health care. Professor Danzon suggested that compensation was already taken care of adequately by private health and disability insurance, combined with the social security disability insurance program. Thus the legal system should be primarily seen as a means of deterrence. Mr. Brown pointed out that the existing insurance system is far from comprehensive, and thus compensation is not assured. If there were a more comprehensive insurance system, Professor Danzon's point would be well taken. Mr. Szanton emphasized again, however, that the system punishes. Even without significant deterrence or the need for additional compensation, society may want to punish the bad actors.

Conclusion   There was a clear consensus among participants that litigation is a key contributor to the rising cost of health care. The decision to place special emphasis on liability litigation seemed appropriate. The speakers and the audience saw such litigation, especially malpractice litigation, as central to the cost problem. Forum participants agreed that little is known about the precise costs and benefits of the tort liability system as it affects health care. Nevertheless, there was a consensus that the system could be made more cost effective by fundamental reform. Substantial agreement occurred on the nature of the problems in the system, as delineated in the papers of Professor Danzon, Professor Mariner, and Mr. Brown. Less agreement occurred on appropriate solutions, especially in the absence of firm data needed to predict the consequences of reforms.

Participants emphasized that better information must be accompanied by greater understanding of the issues by the public. Then the necessary decisions about basic values can be made. Without societal consensus on goals, it is difficult to make changes that will lower the level of litigation. The Brookings Institution hopes that this volume will contribute to better understanding of the role of litigation in raising health care costs and to the development of a new consensus on the proper relationship between the legal system and the health care system.

The Federal Government's Perspective on Litigation and Health Care Costs

ANN T. HUNSAKER

ALTHOUGH THE federal government's interest in health care is clearly delineated by statute and does not extend into all of the facets of health care delivery systems in this country, the government is indisputably a player of major proportions. In fact the federal government is responsible for more than 40 percent of the expenditures made for health care in this country.

Prime Minister Pierre Trudeau once said that for Canada, being a neighbor of the United States is like sleeping with an elephant—when it moves, you know it's there.

I am sure I don't need to remind those of you who are a part of this nation's health care delivery system that when the federal government acts in health care regulation, it will often have an impact on the way you do business.

When the medicare and medicaid programs were first enacted and in their fledgling stages, the health care system that Congress designed was one that focused heavily upon the relationship between government and the individual—between the then Department of Health, Education, and Welfare and the beneficiary under medicare, and between state government and the recipient under the medicaid program.

Disputes, if they arose, were primarily between those parties and were largely concerned with eligibility for program benefits and services. Disagreements between providers of services and the government that would later come to dominate health care litigation were almost nonexistent. Indeed, the government expended great effort during those early years in just finding ways to entice providers to participate in this new health care venture. The courts were busy, but their dockets were not filled with matters relating to the medicare and medicaid programs.

But something happened. At first gradually, and then with great acceleration, perceptions changed as to what constituted a dispute and how the courts might be used as a vehicle to force the government to share not only its policymaking power but its financial resources as well.

11

*The courts
and
complications*

There are many reasons for the explosion of litigation in the health care field, although I am not certain that historical lessons necessarily point to solutions. Certainly the aging of our population, prospects of ever-increasing longevity, the skyrocketing cost of technology, and a gradually diminishing pool of dollars to meet an increasing demand have played their part in explaining why disputants turn to the courts. They seek solutions there even though the courts are not the best branch of government to resolve certain issues.

Moreover, for purposes of the medicare and medicaid programs, the relationship between provider and government, and beneficiary or recipient and government, is governed by the Social Security Act—legislation whose Byzantine construction has been referred to by Justice Henry J. Friendly as "almost unintelligible to the uninitiated."[1]

Litigation is often a fair possibility under the clearest of statutes; under complex statutes, it is a certainty. It is no wonder then that with billions of dollars at stake annually, a perhaps not-so-willing judiciary is often asked to interpret matters of withering complexity.

In fact, some disputes seem to require a battalion of attorneys and support staff simply to explain to the court what the problem is. Consequently, it is not surprising that the courts have become an unwilling partner in the creation of health care policy.

The fact that the courts have become important in the design of health care policy has clearly had an impact on the formulation of this policy at the federal level. Health care policy is still fashioned on the merits of the issue as it arises. Decisions affecting providers and beneficiaries are frequently conceived with an eye to the possible reaction of the courts. The legal arguments that can be made in support of a desired policy objective are also considered.

The thirty attorneys working under my supervision spend virtually all of their noncourtroom time assisting the Health Care Financing Administration in developing policies that are lawful and defensible, and they try to anticipate the legal challenges that almost inevitably draw those policies into the courtroom.

From the federal government's perspective, then, health care litigation weaves a pattern far more complicated than the legal arguments that publicly articulate the issues of each case. It is too simple to say that providers and program beneficiaries on the one

1. *Friedman* v. *Berger*, 547 F.2d 724, 727 (2d Cir. 1976).

hand, and government on the other, have different views on the law. Rather, providers and beneficiaries sometimes see one another as advocates for different ends of the same political and economic spectrum. Providers and beneficiaries are concerned with maximizing revenues from what they perceive to be a dwindling financial reserve, both corporate and personal. The government wants to make sure that its own limited financial resources do not contribute unnecessarily to health care costs in this country.

The Hill-Burton Act and the medicare statute

There are two recent groups of cases that in many ways illustrate the competing pressures I have described.

The first involves the government's experience in litigating the Hill–Burton free-care issue with numerous hospitals around the country. The problem highlighted by these cases stems from the relationship between two statutes: one enacted almost twenty years ago and the other almost forty years ago.

Stated simply, the Hill–Burton Act imposed upon hospitals an obligation to provide free care to those who could not afford to pay for hospital care. In exchange hospitals would reserve government funds to finance the construction and modernization of hospital facilities.

Although the act required its recipients to provide a reasonable volume of services to the indigent, the act did not specify who would ultimately pay for the free care. Would it be the hospitals, the local community, or private contributions? Regulations of the Surgeon General indicated that Hill–Burton free care could be paid from any of these sources and could include the use of public funds.

The medicare statute, enacted twenty years after Hill–Burton, provided for reimbursement of the reasonable cost of needed medical care to medicare beneficiaries, including indirect costs. The cost of charity care, however, was not covered. To some extent, the charity care exclusion was not much of an issue during the early years of the medicare program, because health care costs had not yet taken off, and because many hospitals were ignoring their Hill–Burton free-care obligations.

In the early 1970s, dual pressures of spiraling medical costs and initiatives to enforce more strictly the free-care requirement became evident. Hospitals were now faced with a threefold problem: increasing numbers of patients who had no financial resources; a government that was enforcing statutory requirements; and the consequent strains of looking for revenues to offset the ever-increasing cost of providing free care.

Faced with these pressures, hospitals turned to the medicare program. They argued that providing Hill–Burton free care was a part of the cost of doing business, and that since there was a benefit to medicare patients in the newly constructed or modernized hospital facilities, medicare should pay its share of the cost of these services as an indirect cost.

The Department of Health and Human Services disagreed. It responded that the government was barred by statute from paying for the cost of care for persons ineligible for medicare benefits, whether those costs were direct or indirect. In fact, the persons on whose behalf the hospitals were claiming costs were ineligible under the medicare program. Moreover, the care provided to indigent persons was clearly charity care, and federal regulations barred reimbursement of that care.

Left to the courts to resolve, the Fifth Circuit rendered a decision in 1981 that the government believes badly misconstrued both the scope of medicare reimbursement and the intent of the Hill–Burton program. In *Presbyterian Hospital of Dallas* v. *Harris,* the court concluded that construction funded through Hill–Burton indirectly benefited medicare patients, thus qualifying the hospital for reimbursement of its free-care costs.

In reaching its conclusion the court never did squarely confront the basic premise of the Hill–Burton statute and its regulations that require hospitals to provide a certain level of "uncompensated services" to indigents. The Department of Health and Human Services believed that for the federal government to pay hospitals for the costs of these services through the medicare program would render the hospitals' Hill–Burton obligations meaningless. Under the court's decision, however, a hospital's free-care obligation would now be financed by the federal government.

Legal solutions versus legislative solutions

Although the government has consistently prevailed in more recent Hill–Burton cases, the *Presbyterian Hospital* decision exposed a fundamental flaw in the development of health care policy. That is, the important matter of Hill–Burton free care was left to the courts to resolve and not to Congress.

Legal arguments aside, the Hill–Burton litigation arose because Congress did not anticipate highly significant policy issues: given the interrelationship of two major pieces of legislation—the Hill–Burton and medicare acts—what was meant by free care, and who should shoulder the burden of providing free care to indigents? Should one government program serve to subsidize a hospital's statutory obligations under another?

Although the government believed the Hill–Burton and medicare acts to be reasonably clear on these issues when read together, obviously not everyone agreed.

It was left to the courts to sift through complicated issues of statutory construction in an attempt to reconstruct congressional intent. The result was a decision that could have signaled a leap in federal health care costs that was unanticipated, and unintended, by Congress.

In 1982 Congress amended the medicare statute to explicitly preclude the reimbursement of Hill–Burton free-care costs. Even this enactment is a double-edged sword. Certainly, on the one hand, it reinforces the department's position. On the other hand, it has spawned a new round of litigation focusing on the constitutionality of applying the new amendment to cost years preceding its enactment.

Like the Hill–Burton litigation, the department's ongoing litigation over the reimbursement under medicare malpractice insurance premiums poses a classic illustration of health care litigation as a means to relieve the stress of a costly health care delivery system.

Malpractice, the hospital industry, and the role of medicare

In the days following the enactment of the medicare program, the issue of malpractice was not a high priority for the hospital industry. Although the doctrine of charitable immunity was beginning to erode, malpractice litigation was sparse, and most of it focused on physicians, not hospitals. Malpractice insurance premiums in a typical 200-bed hospital might have run about ten dollars per year per bed, amounts that constituted a minor item in a hospital's general and administrative costs.

Within ten years, however, the complexion had been altered significantly. Hospitals were now often a target of malpractice suits as long as the challenged conduct occurred within the hospital. Hospitals were sharing malpractice responsibilities and liabilities with physicians. Hospitals found that they were not immune from the upward swing in litigation that was spreading throughout society and making the pursuit of civil damages a growth industry.

As malpractice awards grew in size and number, so did malpractice insurance rates. Now some hospitals could not get insurance coverage at any price, and it was not unheard of for a facility to pay as much as $10,000 per bed per year. A once insignificant fraction of a hospital's cost had become a cost of major proportion.

The trend did not escape the notice of the department. Questions were raised about whether the medicare program was sharing properly in the cost of malpractice insurance, and, if not, what changes might be appropriate. Since the inception of the program, the department had reimbursed malpractice insurance premiums in much the same way that it had for many other costs under the program—that is, by application of a utilization ratio of medicare patients to the total patient population.

Upon study, however, it became clear to the department that medicare patients were, on the whole, responsible for a very small proportion of a hospital's malpractice losses. Medicare beneficiaries have shorter life expectancies and generally a smaller earning capacity. Thus medicare beneficiaries posed a significantly lower risk to hospitals. Yet, the medicare program was reimbursing malpractice premiums costs as if the risks for all of a hospital's patients were exactly the same.

In the face of the rise in the costs of malpractice insurance, it is hardly surprising that the department's malpractice regulation, adopting the loss-ratio rather than utilization-ratio approach to reimbursement, was met by a less than enthusiastic hospital industry. I will not attempt to characterize the hospital industry's position—I am sure a number of you could do that better than I—but whatever the merits of the arguments in its behalf, the industry viewed the malpractice regulation as another step toward the curtailment of revenues when no prospect of a reduction in hospital costs was in sight.

The question for the industry was what to do about it. In the broad sense, there were two options: appeal to Congress for a legislative solution, or resort to the courts.

Although I am hardly privy to the strategic deliberations of the hospital industry, I suspect that a legislative solution was not considered realistic. Fifteen years ago Congress might have been more sympathetic to the protection and advancement of institutional health care providers, but now Congress is clearly more selective in judging where federal revenues are most properly spent. Thus the competition for limited revenues and the prevailing perception that there are limits to the problems that the federal government can redress through financial contribution made legislative relief for hospitals most unlikely.

So, once again the health care industry turned to the courts to resolve a fundamental policy question. To what extent should the federal government share a hospital's costs of attempting to protect its assets from potentially staggering malpractice losses? I am not suggesting that the legal arguments on either side of this continuing dispute are not substantial or are merely a smoke screen for more basic complaints about our system of health care financing. The arguments are substantial, and there is much at stake for both sides.

But although the dispute can be translated into legal terms suitable for resolution by the courts, I question whether the courts are the most effective or desirable forum for resolving an issue of this type. Certainly to gauge from the aggregate of the district court decisions thus far, the courts are clearly having difficulty in finding a consistent way to ascribe legal conclusions to issues of equity.

Some observers have asked whether or not the malpractice issue is a significant one. Certainly the medicare program's reimbursement of the costs of malpractice insurance is only one element of a much larger issue that concerns the federal government. However, I can tell you that at least from the government's perspective, the issue is significant. Currently about fifty-five cases that directly challenge the validity of the malpractice regulation are in litigation. New cases are appearing at the rate of about two to three a week. I recently heard that the hospital industry thus far has spent at least $4 million in attorneys' fees in pursuit of this litigation.

The department estimates that in fiscal 1984 alone, approximately $730 million in medicare funds are at stake on this issue. These are sizable numbers and, I suspect, an indicator of significance not only to the medicare program in particular, but to the health care industry as a whole.

The medicaid program
In the medicaid program, the federal government generally gets hit from all sides. The government gets sued by the states, by providers of medicaid services, and by participants—sometimes all in the same lawsuit. States generally sue the federal government over the amount of federal matching money in this state-administered program. These cases usually have been fully briefed and argued at an administrative level through the department's Grants Appeal Board. Once in court, the department's position is sustained about 85 to 90 percent of the time.

Providers of services paid for by medicaid frequently sue the federal government for approving amendments to state plans of operations that do not reimburse the provider at a rate that the provider feels is acceptable. The federal government requires only an assurance from the state that the amount of reimbursement under medicaid is reasonable. Every time the federal government has been drawn into these disputes, the role of the federal government in relying on state assurances has been sustained.

Some states are initiating medicaid reimbursement plans that will reduce the medicaid dollars going to health care providers. In discussing those plans with representatives, I have been told more than once that they do not intend to initiate a legal challenge to medicaid cutbacks. Why? They know that the state could initiate other cutbacks that could cost them more money. I think it is a good sign that providers are finally taking a realistic look at the limited public fisc.

Medicaid participants sue the federal and state governments to broaden eligibility requirements and increase medicaid coverage of health services. Every time the Supreme Court has reviewed the federal government's position on medicaid eligibility, as in the *Schweiker* v. *Gray Panthers* and *Schweiker* v. *Hogan* cases, and federal funding of services, as in *Harris* v. *MacRae,* the abortion funding case, the government's position has been upheld.

In these cases, the Supreme Court gave great deference to the department's interpretations of statutes and to the authority of Congress to limit payment for certain services. Unfortunately, the federal government's victories have not stemmed the tide of the lawsuits in this area.

Litigation and the implementation of policy

The onslaught of health care litigation, typified by the malpractice regulation cases, has taken its toll and provided some lessons. Litigation can serve effectively to delay the implementation of federal health care policy. Litigation is also a time-consuming, laborious, and often plodding process that can give an aggrieved provider years of reprieve from an adverse reimbursement decision.

There are, for example, a number of active cases that focus on cost determinations dating back ten years. Lawyers in our office spend what I think is a disproportionate amount of time defending sound policy decisions made long ago, rather than focusing on current and future issues that face the health care industry.

It is understandable then that a closer examination of what kinds of disputes and what kinds of individuals or providers should have access to the courts to redress their grievances is occurring. The issue of jurisdiction, once seen appropriate only in bar exams and law review articles, has become a major battleground of the 1980s. Jurisdictional issues now dictate how cases are presented, reflecting an increasing body of case law that is making the rules on who has access to the courts and what issues can be considered by the courts.

Under part B of the medicare program, for example, the government has always argued that judicial review is foreclosed to disputes over the amount of benefits due from the medicare program. During the early years of the program, the government was usually successful. As the program expanded, however, small individual claims were joined by far greater claims generated by institutional providers and suppliers. For example, providers of services to the end stage renal disease program sued for greater reimbursement under part B. Courts became more and more reluctant to find that the Social Security Act did not permit access to the courts for the adjudication of these claims. However, in a 1982 decision, the Supreme Court in *Erika* v. *United States,* held that indeed there was no judicial review of part B benefit determinations.

Just as *Erika* was a landmark decision that the government felt would put to rest an entire era of litigation, it served also as a harbinger for a new wave of cases that test *Erika*'s limits and thereby test the government's effort to seek appropriate limits on the judicial review of part B claims.

Thus *Erika*'s shadow cases arise that attempt to distinguish between challenges to the method of payment as opposed to the amount of payment; and, more significantly, cases arise that focus on procedural challenges to ostensibly "enforce lawful conduct" under part B as distinct from a direct claim for monetary reimbursement. The same disputes that the Supreme Court has said are not subject to judicial review have returned to the courts in the form of clever characterizations through legal gymnastics. The Supreme Court will be ruling soon on one case and has been asked to rule on another. I hope the Court will untangle some of the complexities created by the lower courts by exploring once again what disputes Congress intended to be subject to judicial review.

In the same term that the Supreme Court decided *Erika* in the government's favor by a nine-to-zero vote, it decided the *McClure* case in the government's favor by nine to zero.

In *McClure,* medicare beneficiaries initiated a broad-based constitutional challenge to the department's procedure of contracting with carriers to review decisions to pay claims under part B of the medicare program—the hearing process. Noting that the due process requirements are flexible and call for such procedural protections as the situation demands, the Supreme Court rejected plaintiffs' arguments. Clearly the Supreme Court signaled its intent that review of a decision does not require a full-blown fair hearing to fairly protect everyone's interests.

If the court had ruled otherwise, there would have been a tremendous impact on the cost of administrative litigation. A full hearing on denial of a $200 part B claim could have cost $2,000. Thus it would have been less financially burdensome for the government to wrongfully pay a claim.

Apart from controlling the number of part B disputes that reach the courts through the use of jurisdictional defense, it is noteworthy that Congress has spoken clearly on the scope of administrative and judicial review under medicare's new prospective payment system (PPS) for hospitals.

Considering that judicial review is almost uniformly perceived as a right to be zealously protected, it is striking that Congress drew the line where it did under PPS. The appeal procedures available under PPS are noteworthy much more for what they do not include than for what they do include. Thus while the hospital may dispute application of the principles that underlie the new rate system, it may not challenge the principles themselves, either administratively or judicially. Under PPS, the department has established 468 diagnostic-related groups (DRGs). When a medicare patient is admitted to the hospital, he or she will be placed in one of the DRGs, for which the hospital will receive a fixed payment.

A hospital may challenge a decision to place a particular case within one DRG, as opposed to another, but it may not challenge the underlying legitimacy or reasonableness of the DRG itself. Nor may a hospital challenge the government's decisions on costs for a diagnosis as a result of its comparison, or weighting, with respect to other diagnoses covered under the system. Budget neutrality, which assures that hospital-specific payments under the new system will not exceed what payment levels would have been under the old reimbursement-cost system, is also beyond the reach of a hospital's potential attack.

The thread common to each of these factors—the establishment of DRGs, their weighting, and budget neutrality—is that they define the system itself; they are, in effect, the foundations upon which the system rests prospective payments. If challenges were allowed to these primary elements of the system, a nightmarish prospect of the continual recalculation of every hospital's prospective rate could become a reality, destroying not only the prospective character of the system, but the system itself. Clearly, Congress did not wish this to occur.

It is too early to do anything more than speculate about the impact that these new limits will have on the flow of litigation under PPS and ultimately on the costs of the health care system borne by the medicare program. One thing is certain, however: hospitals, their consultants, and their counsel will be assembling their combined creativity to seek out, identify, and use every opening the system provides to pursue what they believe to be their best interests. I find it unlikely that such efforts will be devoted to seeking the reduction of payments under the new system.

Conclusions   Notwithstanding the avalanche of health care litigation in recent years, I am hardly so cynical or immersed in the government's perspective as to reject the notion entirely that this litigation can sometimes benefit the development of health care policy.

In theory, litigation can serve as a control on arbitrary government action and can in this fashion provide checks and balances on improper conduct. To this extent, the public good can be served by the public's knowing that government decisions are adequately conceived and properly implemented. But as the financial stakes have grown—as the competing pressures of cost control and an expanding demand for medical care have intensified—the temptations to pursue advocacy at any price have also risen. I sometimes believe that more and more advocacy occurs for the sake of delay—to prolong, by recourse to the courts, the period that inhibits the government from implementing legitimate policy objectives. I do not pretend to always know at what point legitimate advocacy gives way to obstructive behavior, but I do know that this boundary is crossed and has served, in part, to encourage Congress and the department to find ways of limiting the type and number of disputes that reach the courts, an effort that the Supreme Court seems to have encouraged.

Certainly, as health care providers perceive that they cannot take many significant steps without consulting an attorney, the health care bar has become more than just a thriving cottage industry. And as litigation increases, so do costs.

The health care system, striving to provide quality care within budgetary limits that reflect economic realities, presents a delicate balance. The scales reflect the needs of providers and beneficiaries on the one hand and government on the other to achieve sensible health care objectives. The challenge arises in trying to find a way to maintain that balance without a headlong rush to the courts with issues that don't belong there.

Liability Rules and Health Care Costs

DEBORAH J. CHOLLET

IN THIS SOCIETY, people who have been injured, particularly through no fault of their own, are generally compensated. In fact, compensation for injury or loss is a fundamental goal of our tort system. Spreading the risk of injury (and its subsequent economic costs) to members of society more able to bear injury costs and providing incentives to avoid injury underpin society's agreement to compensate the injured.

Injury can occur in the context of most economic transactions. Workers may be injured in the context of their employment. Consumers may be injured in the context of using either products or services. Environmental hazards created in the course of production may threaten the health and welfare of people who are neither producers nor consumers of the product creating the hazard.

During the past twenty-five years the legal and economic literature about compensation and accident avoidance has expanded rapidly.[1] In general, this literature addresses the following concerns:

—How the assignment of liability affects the allocation of resources to production and to injury avoidance;

—How current liability standards stray from standards of optimal resource allocation; and more recently,

—How regulation might be preferred to liability assignment.

Liability and the allocation of resources

In a perfectly competitive world, with small actors and no transactions costs, the assignment of liability does not affect the allocation of resources to production and injury avoidance. The assignment of liability to either the "injurer" or the person who is injured affects the distribution of income between the two[2];

---

1. See Ronald H. Coase, "The Problem of Social Costs," *Journal of Law and Economics,* vol. 3 (October 1960), pp. 1–44. His paper is generally considered the seminal work in the current literature on liability rules and resource allocation.

2. See Koichi Hamada, "Liability Rules and Income Distribution in Product Liability," *American Economic Review,* vol. 66 (March 1976), pp. 228–34.

22

liability assignment in this model does not affect levels of output, levels of precautionary activity, or the resulting level of injury. Given any clear assignment of liability in this model, negotiations occur between people likely to cause injury or damage and people likely to sustain injury or damage. When people likely to cause injury because of their production activity are made liable, expected compensation costs are directly incorporated into the costs of production. When people likely to sustain injury or damage are made liable, they can bribe potential injurers to reduce the levels of production activity that lead to injury or to undertake efficient levels of precautionary activity. When precautionary activity by people likely to sustain injury is efficient, assignment of liability to either party again does not affect allocation of resources.

The perfectly competitive model, however, describes little of the real world. Transactions between people likely to, respectively, do and sustain injury or damage can be costly. Furthermore, the measurement of injury or damage sustained is difficult and often subjective, especially where accidental death or permanent impairment is at issue. Such considerations have led to a common-law system of torts with complex liability rules and uncertain outcomes.

Liability rules   In general, tort liability relies on two alternative rules, or standards: negligence and strict liability. To illustrate the distinction, consider the question of a manufacturer's liability for consumer injury.

Under a negligence rule, the producer may be liable for consumer injury if he or she fails to take reasonable precautions to make the product safe for people who are likely to be exposed to it. A negligence rule focuses on the reasonableness of the producer's conduct as the basis for deviating from the principle of caveat emptor ("let the buyer beware").

In contrast, a strict liability rule might assign liability to the producer (caveat vendor), regardless of the care exercised in designing, manufacturing, or marketing the product. Strict liability generally assigns liability to the people most likely to correctly make decisions about accident avoidance.[3] Strict liability rules, therefore, may invoke considerations of "reasonable foreseeability" or "failure to warn" as a basis for producer liability. Under a strict liability rule a producer has few defenses. In general, they include consideration of the following: proximate cause (Was the product related in a causal way to the plaintiff's injury?); the

3. This definition of strict liability is found in Guido Calabresi, "Optimal Deterrence and Accidents," 84 *Yale Law Journal* 656 (1975).

state of the art (Did the product meet accepted standards at the time it was produced?); contributory negligence (Did the consumer through negligence contribute significantly to the circumstances of injury?); and assumption of risk (Did the consumer know the risk connected with the product's use?).

Because of the transactions costs associated with the tort liability process, compensation for injuries arising from certain circumstances has been removed from the tort system altogether. For example, the workers' compensation system compensates workers for injury sustained in employment without requiring proof of negligence by employers. Some have argued that employers agreed to remove workers' compensation from tort proceedings to forestall the application of strict liability to workers' injuries. Nevertheless, the workers' compensation system assures workers and their dependents of compensation in return for lower compensation levels and employer immunity from tort liability.[4]

Liability and compensation for injury sustained in the consumption of a product or service, as well as injury sustained by people not directly involved as consumers or producers, are still determined in tort proceedings. In general, product liability (that is, liability for injury or damage sustained in the consumption of a product) is governed by a strict liability rule. The application of strict liability to product-related injury has been significant in raising the price and limiting the marketing of many products—including those connected with the production of health care.

In contrast, professional liability (that is, liability for injury or damage sustained in the consumption of a service) is governed by a negligence rule. Such is true of medical malpractice. The application of a negligence standard to medical liability reduces the chance of compensation for medical (or iatrogenic) injury, compared with what might occur under a strict liability rule. As a result, the market price of health care services (excluding consideration of injury costs) is probably lower, and the volume of services delivered is probably higher than might occur under strict liability.[5]

4. Many state courts have waived exclusive resort under workers' compensation laws to allow tort litigation against employers under a doctrine of dual capacity. Tort proceedings based on dual capacity contend that the employer may be strictly liable for employee injury if the employee was injured in using a product manufactured by the employer. Admission of dual capacity in a workers' compensation case allows the employee to sue the employer independent of any workers' compensation award and to receive additional compensation as well as a punitive award.

5. This is basically the same result obtained by Walter Y. Oi, "The Economics of Product Safety," *Bell Journal of Economics and Management Science,* vol. 4 (Spring 1973),

Liability and the health services market

Negligence-based and strict liability rules affect the health services market at virtually every juncture. Certainly, the negligence rule that governs professional liability encourages duplicative, costly, and possibly excessive diagnostic testing by hospitals and physicians. It also probably reduces the incidence of negligent medical practice.

Ironically, however, negligence-based liability for medical injuries may not always improve the safety or success of health care services. By raising the cost of producing health care and, consequently, raising health care prices, the assignment of liability to producers may raise the demand for lesser-quality health care in some circumstances: when consumers are less informed about differences in quality; when the probability of suit from a particular consumer group is low; and when the demand for care is price inelastic.[6] Under these circumstances, the market for health care services may become segmented, with qualitatively different services delivered to different segments of the market. Incidentally, medicare's refusal to pay hospital medical malpractice insurance costs on a prorated basis assumes this kind of segmentation in the market for health care services.

The strict liability rule governing product liability also affects the health services market. The essence of strict liability is not how much precaution (such as testing and market research) is necessary to absolve the producer, but rather, how much precaution assures the product's safe use. This more stringent standard may lead to producers' selectively marketing drugs and medical equipment to certified health care providers. Strict liability may discourage the development of some drugs and equipment for direct use by the public. Selective marketing and product development, in turn, may significantly reduce levels of self-care among the population and reinforce the demand for professional health care services.

When the application of strict liability has threatened the availability of health care, some states have passed laws to protect health care providers from product liability suits. In some states, the application of product liability rules to blood, for example, threatened to impede or curtail the supply of blood provided by hospitals. These states responded with laws that specifically exempt blood (and serum) transfusions from product liability litigation.

---

pp. 3–28; and Walter Y. Oi, "The Economics of Product Safety: A Rejoinder," *Bell Journal of Economics and Management Science,* vol. 5 (Autumn 1974), pp. 689–95.

6. Oi, "The Economics of Product Safety."

In 1979, however, an Illinois appellate court found that hospitals may be strictly liable for injury sustained as a result of x-ray treatments if the hospital fails to adequately warn the patient of the hazards involved. Although the application of strict liability in professional service settings may, in some cases, improve the safety of health care services, it also promises to substantially raise prices for health services.

Insured risk   The risk of product or professional liability is insurable. In both cases, producers are able to purchase market insurance for compensation and litigation costs, if not for punitive damages awarded by the courts. In general, the availability of market insurance should improve the efficiency of resource allocation to production; it should also improve the efficiency of producers' decisions to undertake precautionary activity. When insurance is priced at actuarially fair levels, the availability of insurance (assuming that producers are risk averse) should raise levels of output and decrease precautionary activity to efficient levels.

The pricing of insurance, however, is seldom actuarially fair.[7] As a rule, insurance prices are calculated within broad rate classes. Members of the rate class share characteristics that, often with significant error, are expected to predict the probability and size of successful claims against members of the class. The insurance price that emerges reflects the expected value of successful claims against the mean member of the rate class, plus a loading factor to cover the insurer's administrative expense.

Assigning insurance premiums this way can greatly distort incentives for producers. Among members of the rate class whose expected value of liability is less than the mean, unfair insurance prices inhibit production, potentially reducing the average safety of services or products available in the market. Conversely, members of the rate class whose expected value of liability is greater than the mean are subsidized by the below-mean members of the class. Their level of output is raised and, again, the average safety of services or products available in the market is reduced.

The distortion of insurance prices may also produce adverse incentives at the margin. That is, when changes in the level of a producer's precautionary activity and expected value of liability result in no change, or disproportionate changes, in the price of liability insurance, the assignment of liability for consumers'

7. Although the allocative results of insurance loadings that are proportional to the probability of injury are essentially those that occur with actuarially fair insurance, even this situation may be unrealistic.

injuries no longer provides efficient incentives for the allocation of resources and may seriously reduce product or service safety.[8] The implications of different insurance pricing practices for the optimality of tort liability have not been adequately addressed in the literature.

Alternatives to liability

Several facts seem to predispose society toward reliance on regulation, versus reliance on liability, to control the risk of injury or damage.[9] These include the following:

—Differences in knowledge about risky activities possessed by private parties versus the regulatory authority;

—The possibility that private parties might be incapable of paying fully for harm done;

—The possibility that parties may not face the threat of suit for harm done; and

—The level of administrative costs incurred by private parties and by the public in connection with the use of the legal system versus regulation.

Tort liability for injury in the consumption of goods or services is usually accompanied by some regulation of producers. That is, physicians are certified; and the production and marketing of drugs and equipment must correspond to regulatory standards established by the Consumer Product Safety Commission and the Food and Drug Administration.

Questions about appropriate regulation are among the many suitable at this conference. Are current levels of regulation in conjuction with tort liability acceptable in ensuring safety in health care services, drugs, and equipment? Or, would the problem of rising health care costs, fueled by litigation costs, be better addressed by changing the current mix of liability and regulation? Closer regulation of providers (e.g., suspending the licenses of providers involved in repeated or multiple malpractice litigation) and more stringent testing standards for drugs and medical equipment should be considered important options for reducing litigation costs in the health care market.

8. The production of safety in response to medical malpractice insurance price distortions is empirically assessed in Deborah Chollet, "Insured Liability for Injury: The Production of Safety in Medical Care," paper presented to the Risk Theory Seminar of the American Risk and Insurance Association (Columbus, Ohio, March 1982).

9. In particular, see Steven Shavell, "A Model of the Socially Optimal Use of Liability and Regulation," Working Paper 1220 (New York: National Bureau of Economic Research, 1983); and "Liability for Harm versus Regulation of Safety," Working Paper 1218 (New York: National Bureau of Economic Research, 1983).

The Medical Malpractice System: Facts and Reforms

PATRICIA M. DANZON

As AN ECONOMIST, I am concerned with the cost effectiveness of the malpractice system in performing its dual functions of deterrence of medical negligence and compensation of the injured patients. In response to the widespread criticism of the current system and the search for reform, I would like to stress the following points:

—The malpractice system is costly and imperfect, but these defects are often exaggerated.

—The cost of malpractice—the real social cost of injuries occurring because of medical negligence—is many times greater than the more visible costs of malpractice insurance premiums and wasteful defensive practices. Therefore in considering reform, the deterrence of malpractice must be considered at least as important as the cost of malpractice claims.

—The current negligence or fault-based approach is worth retaining as a system of quality control—a deterrent to malpractice.

—The malpractice system can be made more efficient by several specific reforms, which I shall discuss.

—A no-fault approach, such as that embodied in S. 2690 (the Alternative Medical Liability Act), could be a disaster. Restructuring the medical liability system solely to provide more extensive compensation is not worthwhile. Compensation can be achieved more efficiently and more equitably through existing insurance programs.

Defects of the malpractice system are exaggerated

Malpractice insurance. The allegation that malpractice insurance is a significant cause of the high and rising cost of health care is exaggerated. From 1975 to 1982 malpractice insurance premiums rose roughly 73 percent, while the cost of physicians' services rose 92 percent and the cost of a hospital room rose 130 percent. Overall, malpractice insurance premiums account for roughly 1 percent of the $350 billion health care bill. For physicians, malpractice insurance premiums average between 3 percent and 4 percent of their gross income, ranging from 3 to 4 percent for

28

general practitioners to 5 to 7 percent for high-risk surgical specialties.[1] These percentages have increased only slightly since 1970.

The recent round of increases in malpractice insurance rates follows several years of little or no increase. There is currently no general lack of availability of insurance except in states in which rates are heavily regulated to levels that insurance carriers deem inadequate for the risks involved. Similarly, the availability crisis of the mid-1970s was largely the result of regulation. Price controls in any market discourage supply and lead to shortages. The only difference in insurance markets is that the resulting shortage is called an availability crisis.

Defensive medicine. Defensive medicine is rarely precisely defined and has never been reliably estimated. I shall define defensive medicine as any waste of resources (net excess of costs over benefits) that results from physicians changing their patterns of medical practice in response to the threat of liability. There is no doubt that many tests and treatments are performed that are not cost effective—the costs exceed the expected benefits. But most of this is not defensive medicine. It is the result of the incentives for overutilization built into the traditional fee-for-service system of health insurance. Prospective payment or capitation-based reimbursement for health care, in which payment is determined in advance and is independent of the number of services performed, would do far more to eliminate excessive utilization than would abolition of liability for malpractice.

On the other hand, behavior by physicians that is correctly ascribed to concern over liability is not pure waste. From an economic standpoint, the purpose of the malpractice system is to influence incentives for physicians to take appropriate levels of care. No doubt for most physicians, most of the time, the threat of liability is not necessary. Professional ethics and ordinary standards of human decency lead them to act as perfect agents for their patients to the extent that they can. But financial incentives cause conflict. A physician who skimps on taking history, or who treats a patient that he or she is not really qualified to treat, can enjoy a higher income or more leisure. The malpractice system is designed to offset these conflicting incentives. A recent survey shows that 36 percent of physicians report spending extra time with their patients; 45 percent refer more cases to other physicians;

1. Jane Su White, "Practice Expenses: Has All the Fat Been Trimmed?" *Medical Economics* (November 8, 1982), p. 130.

and 57 percent maintain more detailed records.[2] Spending more time with patients, referring difficult cases—these are precisely the types of increased care that the malpractice system is intended to encourage.

An erratic lottery? The allegation that the tort system is an erratic lottery is exaggerated. An analysis of the disposition of malpractice claims shows that the courts and the settlement process follow the legal precepts of negligence law to a fair degree.[3] More than 90 percent of claims are settled out of court. Two-thirds are closed within two years of filing. On average, claims settle for 74 percent of their potential verdict (the expected award, had the plaintiff pursued the case to verdict and won). Some of the tort reforms enacted in response to the last crisis have indeed made a difference. In particular, caps on awards and mandatory reduction of awards by the amount of collateral benefits (other sources of insurance) have significantly reduced verdicts and settlements in states that have enacted such changes. In general, one obtains a very biased perception of the malpractice system as a whole from the few highly publicized but atypical cases that win huge jury verdicts. These cases are litigated precisely because they involve unusually difficult issues and severe loss.

The real cost of malpractice   The visible costs of the malpractice system—insurance premiums, defensive practices—are small compared with the less visible but far larger costs of malpractice—the injuries that occur because of medical negligence. A 1974 study by the California Hospital Association and California Medical Association showed that roughly 1 in 126 hospital admissions results in an injury because of medical negligence.[4] I estimate that at most, 1 in 10 of these injured patients filed a claim, and at most, 1 in 25 received compensation through the tort system. A rough estimate of the cost of these injuries is $24 billion, or ten times the cost of malpractice insurance premiums.[5] It is surely worth incurring some expense to reduce this incidence of injury occurring because of negligence.

2. Stephen Zuckerman, "The Costs of Medical Malpractice," *Health Affairs,* vol. 3 (Fall 1984), p. 128.

3. Patricia M. Danzon and L. A. Lillard, "Settlement Out of Court: The Disposition of Medical Malpractice Claims," 12 *Journal of Legal Studies* 345 (1983).

4. California Medical Association and California Hospital Association, *Report on the Medical Insurance Feasibility Study* (San Francisco, Calif.: Sutter Publications, 1977).

5. This assumes that, of a total of $2.4 billion of malpractice premiums, 40 percent represents compensation of injured patients who account for one twenty-fifth of all injuries resulting from malpractice.

Malpractice as a system of quality control

How many injuries are actually deterred is unknown, but it is possible to estimate the percentage reduction in the rate of negligent injury that is required to justify incurring the costs of litigating over fault. Using the 1974 estimate that 1 in 10 incidents of negligence leads to a claim and 1 in 25 receives compensation, only a 4 percent reduction in the rate of negligent injury is required to justify the costs of the tort system. If the rate of compensation per negligent injury is currently, say, twice as high as it was in 1974, then an 8 percent reduction in the rate of negligent injury would be required. Similarly, if the tort system entails significant costs other than the litigation costs considered so far—such as defensive medicine, public costs of operating the courts, time, and psychic costs of litigation to patients and providers—then the deterrence benefits would have to be higher. On the other hand, to the extent that the compensation received by victims through tort understates their willingness to pay for injury prevention, the deterrence necessary to justify the system is less. This rough calculation suggests that if the number of negligent injuries is, generously, 20 percent lower than it otherwise would be, because of the incentives for care created by the malpractice system, the system is worth retaining, despite its costs. If such estimates do not seem implausible, the fault-based approach is worth retaining.

It is often argued that the malpractice system does not and cannot deter because what is called malpractice is typically an error of judgment that would not be avoided by being more careful. This claim is belied by the evidence. The California study concluded that problems of performance, rather than purely judgmental issues, are overwhelmingly responsible for the medical injuries that occur in hospitals.[6] Similarly, improper performance is the most common allegation in malpractice claims.[7]

Admittedly, there are other mechanisms of quality control—licensure and accreditation, peer review, and other practices. They are useful, but they cannot monitor every patient-physician encounter. The advantage of the tort system is that it provides a continual, ongoing system of "regulation by incentives." And it does not rely on enforcement by the medical profession, which, like any other profession, is notoriously reluctant to police its own members. To illustrate, in California in 1976, there were

6. California Medical Association and California Hospital Association, *Report on the Medical Insurance Feasibility Study,* p. 62.

7. National Association of Insurance Commissioners, *Malpractice Claims,* vol. 2, no. 2 (Brookfield, Wisc.: National Association of Insurance Commissioners, 1980), p. 455.

1,500 paid malpractice claims, but only six disciplinary actions for incompetence or gross negligence.

Reforms

The tort system could be improved by the following reforms:[8]

Awards. Awards for damages should be restructured to resemble more closely the insurance that people buy voluntarily. After all, in its compensation function, the tort system is simply a form of compulsory insurance, which people are required to buy when they buy health care. When faced with the choice—and the bill— most people do not buy insurance against pain and suffering. The tort system should provide compensation for loss of earning capacity (after tax) and for reasonable medical expenses, rehabilitation, and other monetary costs, with special provision for persons with no reported wage loss, such as housewives. Pain, suffering, and other nonmonetary losses are real losses, but money cannot replace them. That is precisely why most people do not choose to insure against them, and the tort system should not force them to. Payment for pain and suffering should be made only in cases of permanent injury and then should be determined by a schedule, based on age and severity of injury.

Payments for economic loss should also be based on a schedule, as in workers' compensation, and should not be determined on an individual, case-by-case basis. Individualizing awards encourages expenditure on litigation, is inefficient insurance (because the amount is uncertain), and adds nothing to deterrence. Payment according to a schedule, based on age and severity of injury, is superior to a single ceiling or cap, which some states have enacted. A uniform limit tends to hit hardest the young, severely injured plaintiff, who has the largest economic loss.

Although reforms of this type are usually advocated as part of a no-fault system, that is not a necessary connection. These changes make sense on grounds of economic efficiency, while retaining the fault-based liability rule. A federal model bill proposing such changes for all branches of tort law, not just medical malpractice, could contribute to overriding the constitutional objections to limiting awards solely to the victims of medical malpractice.

The tort award should not be reduced because of other, collateral sources of insurance coverage. But all private health and disability

8. These are discussed in detail in Patricia M. Danzon, "Tort Reform and the Role of Government in Private Insurance Markets," 12 *Journal of Legal Studies* 517 (1984); and Patricia M. Danzon, *Medical Malpractice: Theory, Evidence, and Public Policy* (Harvard University Press, 1985).

insurers should have rights to seek reimbursement (subrogation) for expenses they incur. Payments under public programs—social security disability insurance, medicare, and medicaid—should be reduced by the amount of the tort award. This would eliminate double compensation while transferring the cost of the injuries to the parties responsible. Assigning costs that way is essential for deterrence.

Periodic payment for permanent injuries should occur through an annuity or trust fund set up by the defendant at time of settlement. This should revert to the defendant (or his insurer) in the event of early death of the plaintiff, minus reasonable payment to his estate. Note that although the payment should be periodic, the amount should be determined at the time of trial or settlement. Periodic payments that are contingent on expenses actually incurred create inefficient incentives to delay rehabilitation and to incur unnecessary expense.

There should be a modest uninsurable fine on the physician or hospital in cases of severe injury caused by gross negligence. This uninsurable fine would replace punitive damage awards. The fine should be paid to the state and used to defray the public costs of the courts.

Statute of limitations. I advocate a short statute of limitations— say, three years for adults, ten years for minors—running from the time of the injury, not from its discovery. (Such a statute is often called a statute of repose.) With rapidly changing technologies, volatile legal rules, and social standards, a long statute of limitations exposes physicians to a severe risk of retroactive application of standards that were not relevant when care was delivered to the patient. Such retroactive application of new standards serves no useful deterrent function, is inequitable, is inefficient insurance, and has contributed significantly to the cost of malpractice insurance and to disruptions in malpractice insurance markets.

Standard of care. The standard to which the physician is held is the "customary practice of physicians in good standing." Unfortunately, customary practice is not necessarily efficient practice because of incentives created by excessive health insurance and fee-for-service reimbursement. There is movement under way toward more cost-effective modes of health care delivery, as the private sector and the public programs experiment with health maintenance organizations, prospective payment, preferred provider networks, and other innovative delivery systems. If these efforts are to succeed in eliminating inefficient practice patterns, they must not be held to the customary norms of traditional fee-for-service medicine. If a physician can show that performing—or omitting—a procedure is justified after weighing the costs, the risks, and the benefits, that cost-benefit evaluation should be recognized as a defense against a malpractice claim.

Contracting out. The tort system mandates a rule of liability, a standard of compensation, and a system of dispute resolution that may well exceed what patients would be willing to pay for, if given the choice. If physicians, hospitals, insurers, and patients enter into contracts that provide for alternative standards of compensation or methods of dispute resolution, such contracts should be honored by the courts, as explicit evidence of the preferences of the parties involved. Some private contracting already exists—for example, some health maintenance organizations' contracts provide for binding arbitration. However, federal legislation explicitly authorizing and establishing guidelines for valid contracts would encourage contracting out, by resolving the ambiguity about the legal status of such contracts.

No-fault could be a disaster

A comprehensive no-fault approach to compensation for medical injury would degenerate into an extremely costly and inefficient system of national health and disability insurance. It would be a disaster. The quasi-no-fault bill currently before Congress (the Alternative Medical Liability Act, S. 2690) has some of the same problems, but to a lesser degree. Under this bill, a defendant could foreclose a civil action by offering to settle, on a no-fault basis, for the amount of the plaintiff's monetary loss and reasonable legal fees, less compensation payable from collateral sources.

If malpractice defendants or their insurers routinely made settlement offers on a no-fault basis, as the bill intends, any patient who suffers an adverse health outcome could file a claim, whether or not negligence had occurred. The number of claims filed could increase at least fiftyfold. This estimate of the potential increase, based on the California data on medical injuries, makes no allowance for invalid claims, that is, claims involving incomplete cure despite the best possible medical care. In fact, I suspect that defendants would frequently not offer to settle but would incur the expense of litigation in order to stop the potential avalanche of claims that would occur if settlement were perceived to be automatic. Thus whether the bill would deliver the promised benefits of fairer and more prompt settlement, for more people, is far from certain.

Several of the goals of S. 2690 could be better achieved by the tort reforms I have outlined. As I argued earlier, eliminating or strictly curtailing payment for nonmonetary loss need not be tied to a no-fault liability rule, nor should it be confined to cases that settle out of court, as S. 2690 proposes. Scheduled awards for monetary loss only would not only eliminate wasteful compensation, but also reduce incentives for litigation and delay, and reduce insurance risk. Prompt settlement could be further encouraged by requiring that the defendant pay prejudgment interest at prevailing market rates, from the date of filing to settlement.

Although the benefits of a quasi-no-fault bill are uncertain at best, S. 2690 would add costs in at least three important ways. First, the proposal to pay future expenses as they accrue is an open invitation for plaintiff delay in rehabilitation and for litigation over what constitutes reasonable expense. Second, wasteful defensive practices may well increase. Even if the stigma of fault is removed, the physician or hospital still incurs an expense in settling a claim and therefore has an incentive to avoid high-risk patients or procedures. Physicians' incentives to avoid high-risk situations would be greatest in the case of uninsured and underinsured patients—those with chronic problems, newborns, the poor, and the elderly who have exhausted their medicare coverage—because the defendant pays only for monetary loss not covered by other insurance. Finally, if the quasi-no-fault system operated as intended, it would effectively act as a form of national catastrophic health and disability insurance. This is not the place to discuss the merits of a national catastrophic insurance program. Suffice it to say that if such a system is deemed desirable, it should be operated and funded as a separate program, not as an add-on to the medical liability system. In fact, social security disability insurance, medicare, and medicaid already provide a substantial safety net for those without adequate private insurance. If the concern is compensation, it would be better to close the holes in this net of programs that serves everyone, rather than devise an expensive add-on program confined to the victims of medical injury.

In conclusion, I believe that the fault-based malpractice system, reformed along the lines I have suggested, is worth retaining as a deterrent to medical negligence. For purposes of additional compensation, there are extensive private and public health and disability insurance programs. If this security net has gaps, they should be closed, but not partially patched through the medical liability system.

A Congressional Perspective

JOHN E. PORTER

I MIGHT SAY I appreciate very much having the opportunity to discuss this important subject with all of you. If you see a smile on my face, it's not only because I'm happy to be here this afternoon, but also because I plan after I leave here to play my first nine holes of golf for the season. I know you doctors and hospital administrators understand that and have a smile on your faces. But you lawyers and academics may not. But, that's my intent. I also appreciate the opportunity to be on the panel with my colleague, Doug Walgren, who's an expert in this area. And I must say that I've just learned that although we're both lawyers, we disagree on this subject. So what you're going to see is a Republican pressing for reform, and a Democrat standing for the status quo, and that isn't seen very often—but here we are.

Let me start by assuming the conference's conclusion—that there are substantial, very substantial, negative effects of litigation on health care costs. I don't know whether you're going to come to that conclusion, I assume you are, but let's start with that as our basic premise.

I will begin by doing some historical tracing. First, this whole problem began when hospitals were no longer subject to the doctrine of charitable immunity. That protected them for the first 120 or so years—a little bit longer than that, actually—of our nation's history. But about 40 years ago, that doctrine was overturned in one case after another. The hospitals became subject to suit. It also used to be very bad form for doctors to go into court and testify against other doctors or a patient to sue the town physician. So doctors weren't very often sued either.

Now, specialization and social mobility, and a far more remote doctor-patient relationship, have changed all of that. So we find hospitals and doctors being sued over and over again. The costs of negligent injuries, which were once borne by the injured, were

Note. John E. Porter, Republican of Illinois, is a resident of Winnetka and represents the tenth district.

then shifted to doctors and hospitals, who were responsible for them. Then through insurance, they were shifted again to the public at large.

Lawyers, of course, began making big bucks on large recoveries. As you know, a jury can often see itself in the role of an injured patient. Insurance companies who stayed in the field began requiring huge reserves for ever-increasing judgments, and premiums for medical care providers went sky high.

History
Doctors then raced down to their state legislatures because personal injury law is under state, not federal, jurisdiction. But then so did the trial lawyers, and only small reforms were made. I'm talking about the middle 1970s now.

Principally, the hospitals and doctors found that they could shift the cost to the premium-paying public or to Uncle Sam, and their panic reduced—or at least they learned to live with it. Doctors formed their own off-shore insurance companies, or in some cases, went bare. I just saw an old friend from high school whose father died. He's a doctor out in Colorado now. His father was a doctor in Illinois, where I come from. He said to me at the time, and I'm the executor of the estate, "Don't give me any assets, I'm going bare out in Colorado." And I said, "Well, that takes a great deal of trust in your wife," who has all of his assets apparently. And apparently also, there's only about 3 percent of doctors who trust their wives that much, because there's only about 3 percent that are currently going bare. That has also been in response to the very high premiums.

Now, in the mid-1980s, there are too many doctors; proprietary hospitals and clinics have sprung up and continue to spring up; HMOs are growing; competition is beginning to show itself in the health care field; and DRGs are really going to test the efficiency of health care providers. Some, I might say, probably won't meet the test and won't survive.

Why has all this come about? Because health care costs, as everyone knows, are the fastest growing part of the federal budget, growing 16 percent in the last fiscal year. And that's in comparison to defense, which grew at a 10 percent rate, and the overall budget, which grew at about a 4.5 percent rate. And as everyone also knows, we have $200 billion deficits out as far as the eye can see.

The medicare trust fund is going broke. Some say it's going to go broke very rapidly; others say it's going to take a little longer. Everyone agrees it's going to go broke if nothing more is done. And that probably will occur sometime in the early 1990s, with some projecting deficits as high as $300 or $400 billion. That will require about a 50 percent increase in medicare taxes, and I must say that I don't see any great rush in the Congress to look to new revenues to solve the problem. Many congressmen are very much aware of two Michigan state senators who recently were recalled for daring to vote for tax increases. So don't think we're going to look at that source to solve the problem.

So we're looking for ways to increase efficiency and also to save money.

We can assume one of the best places to cut costs is to address the problem of medical malpractice. After all, it didn't cost any of us anything, except the injured party, forty or fifty years ago. Why should it cost us anything now? Why can't we go back to what it once was?

Now, hospitals, administrators, and doctors shouldn't jump out of their chairs. We're not going back to the unsued doctor and to the doctrine of charitable immunity. Doctors are going to continue to be subject to being sued. And they ought to be. It helps very much in terms of their own responses and their own responsibility in providing health care to the American people. Besides, I think we've reached the point in our society that every injury, even in the absence of negligence, is likely to be compensated in some way. Whether it's product liability or physician liability, in a sense both have become strict liability. So the old days I think are gone, and what do we do now?

State and federal alternatives

One thing, and it's been suggested by my colleague, is to do nothing, to retain the status quo. The trial lawyers would certainly like that, but frankly, I think I see too much pressure for cost savings and efficiency to give the trial lawyers the status quo. Consider that there is not only a crisis in health care costs, but our research capacities today—capacities to discover new cures, new procedures, new devices, to implant artificial hearts, to transplant livers and pancreases and lungs—will create a demand for all such life-prolonging capacities, a demand that will increase costs even further. In my judgment, we'll be extremely lucky if we can avoid rationing the application of these new discoveries, and avoid deciding who will get a new heart and who will not. That seems to me to be a very real problem in the years ahead and one that is going to put even more pressure on saving money in other parts of the health care field.

So here, as in other areas of health care, the status quo to me looks very unlikely, at least for very long.

A second alternative in addressing the assumed burden of medical malpractice costs on health care is that the states could act in this area. But if you look back in the mid-1970s—and I served at that time in the Illinois General Assembly in our Medical Malpractice Task Force—really very little was accomplished. In Illinois, we put in some pretrial screening and some changes in the rules of evidence, but those were very small, and very little got done. And I think that obtained in most states.

There's also the fact that in the state legislatures, the trial lawyers, if they don't make up half of the membership, have one of the best lobbies in the state capitals. It's very unlikely we can get any great action out of a state with that kind of pressure to bear. So I think that the state as a forum in an unlikely place to see any real action.

Even so, there would remain the problem of even-handed justice, and I think this is the time to address that problem. The question of having a $4 million recovery in one courtroom, and then having a $400,000 recovery in the courtroom next door where there is no discernible difference in the injuries or the facts in the case is justice not even but very uneven. It seems to me that, if we're going to address this entire problem, this is a very good place to address the equity question as well. I don't think these questions can be addressed through any state solution.

The Senate is now considering product liability legislation under which federal standards would be imposed. I think this gives a hint of the possible direction that we might go in addressing this issue.

There's a third alternative: the federal government could act alone with respect to the whole problem of medical malpractice. It could preempt the field. The Supreme Court in the 1940s, in a case I believe Mr. Justice Douglas decided, defined the commerce clause in the Constitution to cover the farmer feeding the corn he grew on his own land to the feed cattle he raised on his own land as an act of interstate commerce. Ever since, we've assumed that anything is in interstate commerce, and therefore subject to Washington's regulation.

Presumably then, we could have a National Control of Medical Malpractice Costs Act, we could preempt state law, have national uniformity and all that goes with it. However, I don't think the trial lawyers are that weak in Washington. Second, I think this approach would be totally out of national tradition. If we don't have precedents any longer, we at least do have traditions.

Some of this direct federal approach, however, is likely to occur, for example, in the area of legislative solutions to the problem of asbestos injuries. We're seeing that right now in Congress. Johns-Manville has had 28,000 individual cases and claims filed against it all across the country in many jurisdictions. In a case like this, we're going to see the federal government preempt the state and provide for a legislative solution to meet the needs of those who are injured. These needs obviously couldn't be met out of the resources of the corporation or its insurance carrier, if indeed it has an insurance carrier. You're going to see some kinds of problems in hazardous wastes addressed legislatively and directly by the Congress, but I don't think you're going to see Congress act alone in a generic way in reference to medical malpractice.

The final alternative is that Congress can pass legislation to give incentives for the states to act. I'm talking here about carrots and then sticks. We're seeing this approach in many areas—the fifty-five-mile-an-hour speed limit is one example of it. Now we're considering having a minimum national drinking age to address the problem of drunk driving in the same way, with incentives to adopt that drinking age in each state across the country.

This approach pervades our federal-state relationship. It isn't anything very new, and we think it's something that can happen here. We could use incentive grants—that would be the carrot. Or we could use a cutoff of medicare or medicaid funds in some percentage—that would be the stick. But whatever type of approach is used, this is a very likely way to address the problem.

What would be the approach, then, in terms of federal legislation in this area? The first one might be based on a workers' compensation model. The principle is that, if an injury is sustained, an individual is entitled to compensation, regardless of negligence. There would be no accusing finger pointed at a hospital or a doctor if that type of approach was used. Uniformity of awards could be more assured under federal standards. Noneconomic losses presumably could be largely squeezed out in such circumstances. At the same time, all of the oxen would not be completely gored since lawyers would still be needed. Although the form would be different and the compensation less, they would be needed. And insurance companies would retain an active role in this field. So, there is a lot of appeal in this kind of approach.

Second, we could try some kind of arbitration system established by federal law. But it's hard to see how this would work much better than a workmen's compensation approach. More oxen would be gored, and matters would still end up in court, because courts have uniformly ruled that binding arbitration is not permissible; it's unconstitutional. Access to the courts must be guaranteed.

Third, we could go to a no-fault model that could be imposed on the states under federal guidelines. This is the approach that I think is most likely, at least right now. Recently, Congressman Henson Moore of Louisiana and Congressman Dick Gephardt of Missouri, a Republican and a Democrat on the Ways and Means Committee, introduced the Alternative Medical Liability Act. This legislation was proposed not as a final word in this area, but as a point of discussion in proposing a solution to a very real problem.

The legislation they have proposed is very modest in scope. It covers only medicare beneficiaries and other federal health programs such as Champus, the federal employees health benefit program and the Veterans' Administration. These are not, as you undoubtedly well know, the areas where most medical malpractice claims come. The elderly, for example, don't tend to sue their doctors or their hospitals. Those big recoveries come in cases of far younger people, where the potential economic loss is far greater. So it's a very modest approach.

The conceptual engineer of this bill was Professor Jeffrey O'Connell, of the University of Virginia Law School, a long-time expert on no-fault legislation. It would work in this way. The patient would notify the health care provider that an injury had occurred. The provider would then have sixty days in which to make a settlement offer. If no offer was made, the patient could then go to court and presumably recover whatever is possible to recover in court today. But if the offer is made—and it needs to cover only the economic loss, not the loss for pain and suffering or attorney's fees or court costs or anything else—then the patient is foreclosed from going to the court, except regarding the reasonableness of the amount. In other words, the question of negligence or liability has been resolved by the making of the offer—that's the no-fault part.

The bill provides for a number of exceptions, which I won't go into now, that would allow a patient in certain circumstances to go to court. But the no-fault concept would be one that would be appealing in a number of different ways. First, there is no accusing finger pointed at negligence of a doctor or a hospital, no untoward publicity; and there is a faster resolution of the problem. Many people wait three, four, or like in my state, five years or more to go to trial and make a recovery. Witnesses die and move away. The difficulty of proving a claim becomes greater and greater. This proposal would lead to faster resolution. No large attorney's fees would be involved. There's an estimate that nationally 42 percent of the amounts paid for medical malpractice claims are in fact turned over directly to the attorneys or to provide for costs of suit. The insurance companies get 30 percent for their overhead. And only 28 cents out of every dollar goes to the victim.

It seems to me that this is a place where reforms are very obviously needed.

Whether it would actually lower costs, and there are many who question whether it would, is something that has to be determined. The bill has been introduced only as a point of departure and a means of discussion of the issue, but I think it is going to receive a great deal of discussion in the months ahead.

A congressional search

What will Congress look for in any approach to solving the problem? Greater uniformity, and therefore greater, more even-handed justice; security, greater protection for the injured person; a lowering of costs through lower premiums, by reducing non-economic losses being compensated, including attorney's fees and court costs; and a faster resolution of conflicts. But I think the most important factor that the Congress is going to look at in addressing this problem is to squeeze out of our health care system the cost of practicing defensive medicine, both the direct costs and the indirect costs. The indirect costs in terms of the loss of physician and hospital time and resources are estimated at 30 percent of our total health care costs. That amounts to more than $100 billion a year, a sum of money well worth saving.

In this entire area as in others in the health care field, the pressures to do something are great and will grow. The most likely approach will be through Congress's mandating a program for the states to adopt with local variation, of course, but under federal standards. In this matter Congress will be guided by experts, including lawyers, who show an understanding of the problem and leadership. I commend all of you for caring about it.

The Potential Impact of Pharmaceutical and Vaccine Litigation

WENDY K. MARINER

LAMENTATIONS over rising health care costs are reaching a crescendo in the United States. For decades public policy focused on improving the quality and availability of health care services. Now the pendulum of public policy debate has swung, if not inexorably, at least decidedly toward concern that the cost of care may be growing at an unjustifiably high rate.[1] At the same time, anxiety is rising about an increased volume of litigation, especially concerning health care services (medical malpractice) and products (product liability). These simultaneous events raise at least two questions important to public policy in the United States. First, are the perceived rates of increase real and justifiable? That is, are they unavoidable or desirable consequences of improvements in the quality and availability of health care or legal services, or do they reflect counterproductive uses of resources? Second, are litigation and health care costs independent and unrelated, or are they somehow causally connected such that increased litigation, for example, generates excess costs for health care services?

While answering the question of whether costs are unavoidable or counterproductive is beyond the scope of this paper, sufficient evidence of the growth in health care costs exists to assume that continued increasing expenditures will adversely affect the nation's capacity to effectively care for the population. Similarly, there is evidence of growth in litigation. But data concerning the proportion of lawsuits affecting health care are sparse and offer fewer clear-cut conclusions.

This paper addresses the question of the relationship between litigation and health care costs by exploring how litigation may affect the development and distribution of pharmaceuticals and vaccines. It presents one strategy for considering the general question of whether a disproportionate amount of health care

1. Bruce C. Vladeck, "Equity, Access, and the Costs of Health Care Services," in President's Commission for the Study of Ethical Problems in Medicine and Biomedical and Behavioral Research, *Securing Access to Health Care*, vol. 3 (Government Printing Office, 1983), pp. 3–17.

costs is attributable to litigation. The strategy consists of identifying and categorizing the types of costs associated with drug and vaccine litigation and determining whether the purposes of such litigation can be achieved in other ways at less cost. When specific data concerning the actual costs of drug and vaccine litigation are available, it is hoped that this framework can be used to assess the need for and likely success of alternatives to litigation.

For purposes of this paper, litigation in regard to drugs and vaccines is confined primarily to cases in product liability. That means disputes about the responsibility of pharmaceutical manufacturers for personal injuries suffered by persons who received a manufacturer's drug or vaccine. Another area of law—drug and vaccine regulation and licensing by the Food and Drug Administration—also has great potential impact on the development and distribution of drugs and vaccines. However, because that potential lies primarily in compliance with administrative requirements for testing and licensing new products and rarely results in litigation, it will not be considered. Rather, this discussion focuses on product liability litigation, including not only litigation in the true sense of lawsuits commenced in court, but also claims made on the basis of product liability theories. Such claims may or may not be settled by the parties or result in a lawsuit.

The conclusions to be drawn from this analysis are that, although litigation is commonly thought to have a negative influence on the production and distribution of drugs and vaccines, data are insufficient to support abandoning tort law as a mechanism for allocating liability and awarding compensation on grounds of cost alone. Differences in the law as applied to drug and vaccine related injuries, as well as the economics of production and the social value of drugs and vaccines, suggest that litigation concerning vaccines may produce costs that threaten the delivery of health care and the protection of public health that do not arise from litigation involving drugs. Accordingly, there is justification for seeking alternative forms of compensating vaccine related injuries. It is not at all clear, however, that effective alternatives will reduce overall costs.

Tort liability for personal injury

In general, litigation is the social mechanism enabling individuals to resolve disputes concerning their respective rights and duties. In theory, a mechanism for enforcing rights and duties serves to ensure that everyone will perform his or her duty as defined by law. Standards of conduct expressed as legal duties establish a minimum level of quality acceptable to society. Thus tort law, which concerns civil wrongs, fosters the dual goals of ensuring socially acceptable behavior and providing compensation to those who are injured because of any failure to conform to required standards. For those who manufacture and sell products such as drugs and vaccines, product liability law defines the standards of care required in the production of drugs and vaccines and assigns responsibility for injury to product consumers. Responsibility for injury embraces the two concepts of compensation and liability, which, although theoretically two sides of the same coin, are distinct notions, occasionally with different implications for public policy. For example, it may be desirable to compensate an injured party for the loss he has suffered. But, perhaps the manufacturer of the product that caused the injury exercised all possible care in making it and should not be responsible (liable) for providing that compensation. Product liability law links compensation to liability, but there may be reasons to separate the two concepts.

Drug Related Injury

Product liability law provides remedies for persons suffering injury because of taking a drug. Today, the most commonly used theories for recovery of compensation for drug related injury are negligence and strict liability, which have effectively displaced theories of warranty.[2] Negligence requires proof of fault on the part of the defendant. The manufacturer may have erred by producing an impure or defective product, or the prescribing physician may have erred by improperly prescribing or administering the drug. In litigation based on negligence theory, a person claiming injury from taking a drug must establish that the defendant committed an error that resulted in the plaintiff's injury. To do this, the plaintiff usually must prove each of the following elements of a cause of action (enforceable claim) in negligence:

—A duty, recognized by law, requiring the defendant to conform to a certain standard of conduct to protect others against unreasonable risks;

—A breach of that duty on the part of the defendant by failing to conform his or her conduct to the relevant standard, such as failing to use reasonable care in the production of a drug;

—Actual loss or damage suffered by the plaintiff; and

—A causal relationship (known as proximate cause) between

2. William L. Prosser, "The Fall of the Citadel (Strict Liability to the Consumer)," 50 *Minnesota Law Review* 791 (1966); Sheila L. Birnbaum, "Unmasking the Test for Design Defect: From Negligence to Warranty to Strict Liability to Negligence," 33 *Vanderbilt Law Review* 593 (1980).

the defendant's conduct (breach of duty) and the resulting injury to the plaintiff.

Potential claims against pharmaceutical companies are limited by the nature of the companies' duties to the ultimate consumers of their products; the rarity of defective drugs; and the difficulty of establishing a causal relationship between the administration of a particular drug and the occurrence of a particular injury.

Strict liability removes the need for proving a breach of duty. Under this theory, which has several variations,[3] a manufacturer is held to be, in effect, an insurer of the safety of a product, even if he has exercised all reasonable care. Section 402A of the Restatement (Second) of Torts imposes strict liability on "one who sells any product in a defective condition unreasonably dangerous to the user."[4] Courts have relied upon the provisions of the Restatement often in deciding cases concerning drug related injury.[5] Comment k to section 402A of the Restatement suggests that, although most drugs (and vaccines) carry risks, they ought not to be subjected to strict liability because, in the current state of human knowledge, it is not possible to produce an absolutely safe drug, one that has no side effects.[6] Continuing controversy over the application of this exception has blurred the distinction between strict liability and negligence in drug cases. Even where strict liability is imposed, the defendant is often said to have committed some "fault."

Drugs are classified as "unavoidably unsafe products" because of their potential risks of side effects and adverse reactions, however remote.[7] Their distribution and use are accepted and justified because of the benefits they confer, which outweigh the small risks of harm. However, if such products are not accompanied by proper directions and warnings of their risks, they are considered "unreasonably dangerous." Warnings must be adequate[8] and not negated by false assurances of safety.[9] Warnings must also be timely, that is, given reasonably promptly after the risk becomes known.[10] The adequacy of the warning, however, is judged as of

3. Joseph A. Page, "Generic Product Risks: The Case Against Comment k and for Strict Tort Liability," 58 *New York University Law Review* 853 (1983).

4. Restatement (Second) of Torts, Section 402A (Chicago: American Law Institute, 1965), pp. 347–58.

5. Richard A. Merrill, "Compensation for Prescription Drug Injuries," 59 *Virginia Law Review* 1 (1973).

6. Restatement (Second) of Torts, Section 402A, comment k, pp. 353–54.

7. Restatement (Second) of Torts, Section 402A, pp. 347–58.

8. *Salmon v. Parke, Davis & Co.*, 520 F.2d 1359 (4th Cir. 1975).

9. *Parke-Davis & Co. v. Stromsodt*, 411 F.2d 1390 (8th Cir. 1969).

10. *Schenebeck v. Sterling Drugs, Inc.* 423 F.2d 919 (8th Cir. 1970).

the date the warning was given, so only risks that were known or should have been known must be disclosed.[11] Liability for injury resulting from such a product depends on who is responsible for issuing the warning and to whom the warning is directed.

Pharmaceutical companies, as manufacturers of "unavoidably unsafe products," have been deemed the proper parties to issue warnings of dangers that are not commonly known or expected in their drugs. For prescription drugs, a manufacturer's duty to warn is directed not to the ultimate consumer but to the prescribing physician, since prescription drugs are not available to consumers without a prescription.[12] The manufacturer might advise the physician of any potential risks of the drug so that the physician can judge whether a particular drug is appropriate for a particular individual. Drug labels and circulars contained in the package, in accordance with licensing requirements, usually convey the necessary warnings.

However, reliance upon package circulars to communicate warnings to physicians has not always precluded assigning liability to manufacturers for adverse reactions to prescription drugs, despite the prescription drug rule. In cases concerning Chloromycetin, a brand name of chloramphemicol, a wide-spectrum antibiotic, several courts have found that manufacturers may incur liability if their promotion and advertisement of the drug effectively negate the written warnings distributed to physicians.[13] For example, the California court in Stevens v. Parke, Davis & Co.[14] held the pharmaceutical company liable for the death of a patient whose bone marrow failed after receiving Chloromycetin. Warnings of the drug's potential for producing blood disorders were included in the literature accompanying the drug and in "dear doctor" letters sent to physicians under Food and Drug Administration (FDA) orders. However, the court found that the company rendered its warning ineffective by vigorously promoting the drug. Among the promotional measures used were personal visits by detail agents who urged use of Chloromycetin without mentioning its risks; advertising in medical journals that contained

11. *O'Hare* v. *Merck & Co.*, 381 F.2d 286 (8th Cir. 1967).

12. *Buckner* v. *Allergan Pharmaceuticals, Inc.*, 400 So.2d 820 (Fla. App. 1981), *pet. den.*, 407 So.2d 1102 (Fla. 1981); *Pierluisi* v. *E. R. Squibb & Sons, Inc.*, 440 F. Supp. 381 (D.C. Puerto Rico 1977).

13. *Salmon* v. *Parke, Davis & Co.*, 520 F.2d 1359 (4th Cir. 1975); *Whitley* v. *Cubberly*, 24 N.C. App. 204, 210 S.E.2d 289 (1974); *Stevens* v. *Parke, Davis & Co.*, 9 Cal. 3d 51, 107 Cal. Rptr. 45, 507 P.2d 653 (1973); *Incollingo* v. *Ewing*, 444 Pa. 263, 282 A.2d 206 (1971); *Love* v. *Wolf*, 249 Cal. App. 2d 822, 58 Cal. Rptr. 42 (1967).

14. 9 Cal. 3d 51, 107 Cal. Rptr. 45, 507 P.2d 653 (1973).

no reference to possible adverse effects; letters sent to the company's detail agents minimizing the drug's risks; and the distribution of free calendars and rulers carrying the name Chloromycetin but no explanation of risks. The court viewed this barrage of advertising as provoking the physician to prescribe the drug inappropriately because he or she relied on promotional materials instead of the actual drug literature.

This and similar cases[15] seem to assume that physicians are so inundated with drug information that they cannot be expected to review drug circular literature for each prescription; rather they will be persuaded to rely on less detailed advertising to assess the merits of particular prescriptions. The more recent practice of including more information about drug risks in advertising materials may render these cases of little practical importance in the future. Moreover, some courts have found that the physician is bound to be familiar with the drug literature in prescribing drugs, regardless of the possible effects of advertising. In *Formella* v. *Ciba-Geigy Corp.*,[16] the physician's failure to read the *Physician's Desk Reference* and order blood tests was found to be the intervening and independent cause of the plaintiff's aplastic anemia resulting from Tandearil prescribed for his arthritis. The drug literature mentioning the need for blood tests provided an adequate warning. Even if the manufacturer was acting negligently in overpromoting the drug, it was not held liable in view of the physician's responsibility.

Physicians are far more susceptible than manufacturers to liability for death or injury resulting from side effects of drugs. The general standards for liability for medical malpractice govern the physician's liability. The medical profession is held to the standard of care, knowledge, and skill ordinarily possessed and exercised by the average qualified practitioner in similar circumstances, taking into account advances in the profession.[17] Therefore, a physician who prescribes or administers a drug must use reasonable skill and care in ascertaining its suitability for the patient. The mere occurrence of an adverse drug reaction does not imply negligence by the physician, since unforeseen reactions are always possible.[18] However, the standard of care obliges a physician to determine whether the patient might be hypersensitive

15. *Mahr* v. *G. D. Searle & Co.*, 71 Ill. App. 3d 540, 28 Ill. Dec. 624, 390 N.E.2d 1214 (1979) (Enovid); *Carmichael* v. *Reitz*, 17 Cal. App. 3d 958, 95 Cal. Rptr. 381 (1971) (Enovid); *Yarrow* v. *Sterling Drug, Inc.*, 263 F. Supp. 159 (D.S.D.), aff'd, 408 F.2d 978 (8th Cir. 1967) (Aralen).

16. 100 Mich. App. 649, 300 N.W.2d 356 (1980).

17. *Brune* v. *Belinkoff*, 354 Mass. 102, 235 N.E.2d 793 (1968).

18. *Campos* v. *Weeks*, 245 Cal. App. 2d 678, 53 Cal. Rptr. 915 (1966).

to the drug and to ensure that the drug is administered properly. Depending upon the circumstances, this may entail taking a careful history of the patient's immunological status and sensitivity to drugs[19]; testing the patient for hypersensitivity to the proposed drug[20]; heeding the manufacturer's instructions for use of the drug[21]; and warning the patient about possible risks of the drug.[22]

Although the bases of physician liability are relatively straightforward, reported decisions of lawsuits are not always consistent in allocating liability. Whether a physician is held liable often depends upon particular state rules governing burdens of proof, evidence, and standards for disclosure in seeking informed consent. For example, states applying the locality rule might find a physician's failure to conduct drug sensitivity tests entirely reasonable in view of the prevailing consensus among local practitioners that such tests are unnecessary. Similarly, if the disclosure of drug risks is governed by a local professional standard of declining to mention risks, a physician would not be held liable for failing to warn of a risk that is not usually disclosed.[23] In states applying the newer standard of disclosure in informed consent cases, which, regardless of professional practice, requires the disclosure of information material to a patient's decision,[24] the likelihood that a physician would be held responsible for failing to warn against possible adverse reactions is greater. The plaintiff's burden of proof is eased in such cases because he has no obligation to present expert testimony to prove that the risk would commonly have been disclosed by the profession. States that follow the professional standard usually require such testimony.

While pharmaceutical companies are most often at lesser risk of liability for individual drug injuries than are physicians, the companies may face new concepts of liability for latent injuries among large groups of drug recipients or their progeny in the future.[25] The DES cases represent a potential exception to the

---

19. *Stokes* v. *Dailey*, 85 N.W.2d 745 (N.D. 1957).

20. *LeBeuf* v. *Atkins*, 22 Wash. App. 877, 594 P.2d 923 (1979); *Mulder* v. *Parke, Davis & Co.*, 288 Minn. 332, 181 N.W.2d 882 (1970).

21. *Incollingo* v. *Ewing*, 444 Pa. 263, 282 A.2d 206 (1971).

22. *Cross* v. *Huttenlocker*, 440 A.2d 952 (Conn. 1981).

23. *Niblack* v. *United States*, 348 F. Supp. 383 (D.C. Colo. 1977); *Tangora* v. *Matanky*, 231 Cal. App. 2d 468, 42 Cal. Rptr. 348 (1964).

24. *Canterbury* v. *Spence*, 464 F.2d 772 (D.C. Cir. 1972). See generally Theodore R. Le Blang, "Informed Consent—Duty and Causation: A Survey of Current Developments," 28 *Forum* 280 (1983).

25. For a discussion of theories of liability concerning drugs and toxic products whose risks may have been scientifically unknowable at the time of marketing, see Joseph A. Page, "Generic Product Risks: The Case Against Comment k and for Strict Liability," 58 *New York University Law Review* 853 (1983).

straightforward application of product liability principles to drug related injuries. These cases involve large numbers of potential plaintiffs whose injuries may become manifest only many years after the drug was prescribed. The DES cases concern possible cancers among women whose mothers received diethylstilbestrol (DES) to prevent miscarriage during pregnancy. In stating a cause of action in product liability, plaintiffs face the difficult (often impossible) requirement of identifying the manufacturer of the drug received by their mothers often twenty years earlier. As a result, they have sought new theories to eliminate this burden and to impose some form of joint liability upon manufacturers of DES.

More than 1,000 suits have been filed against DES manufacturers on behalf of "DES daughters." Few have resulted in reported decisions, and those decisions have differed. Several courts have dismissed the cases or granted judgment for the manufacturers on the grounds that the plaintiff could not prove that the particular defendant's drug caused her injury.[26]

Theories that impose liability on several manufacturers include joint or concerted action liability, alternative liability, and industrywide liability, a generic term covering theories of enterprise and market share liability. Joint liability holds several manufacturers jointly responsible when they take concerted action in bringing a drug to market.[27] In view of the rarity of true concerted action among pharmaceutical houses, however, joint liability is not apt to provide much opportunity for recovery to plaintiffs.

Alternative liability is based on the theory that more than one person negligently exposed a person to risk. All should be held liable even though the injury was only caused by one of them and the one directly responsible cannot be identified. The classic example is the case of *Summers* v. *Tice*,[28] where the plaintiff was shot by one of two hunters who both fired negligently in his direction. Because it was unclear which hunter's bullet hit the plaintiff, the court shifted the burden of proof to the defendant hunters. They would be held jointly and individually liable unless one could prove that the other fired the damaging shot. The notion of alternative liability, although appealing in *Summers* v.

26. *Payton* v. *Abbott Labs*, 437 N.E.2d 171 (Mass. 1982); *Mizell* v. *Eli Lilly & Co.*, 526 F. Supp. 589 (D.S.C. 1981); *Namm* v. *Charles E. Frosst & Co.*, 178 N.J. Super. 19, 427 A.2d 1121 (App. Div. 1981); *Ryan* v. *Eli Lilly & Co.*, 84 F.R.D. 230 (D.S.C. 1979); *Lyons* v. *Premo Pharmaceutical Labs, Inc.*, 170 N.J. Super. 183, 406 A.2d 185 (App. Div. 1979); *Gray* v. *United States*, 445 F. Supp. 337 (S.D. Tex. 1978).

27. *Bichler* v. *Eli Lilly & Co.*, 79 A.D.2d 317, 436 N.Y.S.2d 625 (1981).

28. 33 Cal. 2d 80, 199 P.2d 1 (1948).

Tice, has had little application, largely because there are few cases in which only a few defendants can be identified as including the one party clearly responsible for the plaintiff's injury.[29]

Industrywide liability has greater potential for being used to impose liability on multiple defendants because it does not require a showing either (a) that the defendants acted jointly or in concert, or (b) that each defendant contributed substantially to the injury. A variation on this concept of liability received notoriety in *Sindell* v. *Abbott Laboratories*, in which the Supreme Court of California held that DES daughters stated a cause of action against several manufacturers of DES on a novel theory that it denominated market share liability.[30] The court noted that the defendants had manufactured DES from an identical formula, but the plaintiff, through no fault of her own, could not identify the manufacturer that produced the DES taken by her mother. Under these circumstances, the court shifted the burden of proof, finding that "each defendant will be held liable for the proportion of the judgment represented by its share of that market [in DES] unless it demonstrates that it could not have made the product which caused plaintiff's injuries. . . . Under this approach, each manufacturer's liability would approximate its responsibility for the injuries caused by its own products."[31] Shifting the burden of proof was justified in part by requiring the plaintiff to join as defendants (also sue) the manufacturers who had supplied a substantial portion of the DES at the time it was prescribed. Although this limitation increases the likelihood that one of the companies sued was the one that produced the DES in question, it still subjects multiple defendants to liability even if they did not cause the injury to the plaintiff in the action. The market share theory imposes liability for creating a risk of injury in proportion to the defendants' share of the market for the drug. *Sindell* departs dramatically from traditional principles of negligence by providing a basis for recovery against manufacturers that may not have directly caused the damage for which recovery is sought. At the same time, *Sindell* may be a difficult precedent to apply in non-DES cases. It requires a plaintiff to identify and sue all manufacturers that produced a substantial share of the marketed product,

29. But see *Hall* v. *E. I. DuPont de Nemours & Co.*, 345 F. Supp. 353 (E.D.N.Y. 1972), using alternative liability, joint liability, and notions anticipating market share liability to require defendant manufacturers of blasting caps to bear the burden of proof of identifying the party responsible for marketing blasting caps that exploded and injured thirteen children.

30. 163 Cal. Rptr. 132, 607 P.2d 924, *cert. den.*, 449 U.S. 912 (1980).

31. 607 P.2d at 949.

which may create a major burden in litigation from the plaintiff's perspective. *Sindell* also seems limited to cases in which the defendants engaged in identical activities that created qualitatively identical risks, a relatively rare event.

Vaccine Related Injury

Litigation concerning injuries attributable to vaccines has precipitated more concern among both pharmaceutical companies and consumers than drug litigation has. Although the principles of product liability apply equally to drugs and vaccines, several court decisions have expanded the potential liability of manufacturers of vaccines beyond that ordinarily imposed in cases concerning drugs. Manufacturers of vaccines, like those of drugs and other "unavoidably unsafe products," have a duty to warn recipients of risks inherent in the vaccines. Under the prescription drug rule, vaccine manufacturers were originally held responsible to issue warnings to the physician who prescribed a vaccine. An exception to this rule was created for persons who suffered adverse reactions to vaccines received in mass immunization programs because such persons do not ordinarily have the vaccine specifically "prescribed" for them by a physician.[32] In the absence of the "individualized medical judgment" of a physician, vaccine consumers are entitled to receive information about the risks, as well as the benefits, of the vaccine to help them decide whether to undergo vaccination. Thus the manufacturer must ensure that the warning is given directly to the consumer, rather than to the physician.

Cases involving the oral poliomyelitis vaccine, which carries a remote but real risk of causing polio in those who are vaccinated or in contacts of vaccinees, exemplifly the expanded duty to warn. In the celebrated case of *Reyes* v. *Wyeth Laboratories*,[33] the plaintiff's infant daughter contracted polio shortly after being vaccinated with oral polio vaccine at her parents' request. A public health nurse in a county-operated clinic vaccinated the infant during a local polio epidemic. Wyeth, the vaccine supplier, argued that under the prescription drug rule, it was entitled to rely on the Texas Department of Health, which sponsored the immunization program, to provide any necessary warnings. Although the administering nurse had read Wyeth's package insert, she did not pass any warning on to Reyes. The United States Court of Appeals

---

32. *Davis* v. *Wyeth Laboratories*, 399 F.2d 121 (9th Cir. 1968); *Stahlheber* v. *American Cyanamid Co.*, 451 S.W.2d 48 (Mo. 1970).

33. 498 F.2d 1264 (5th Cir.), *cert. den.*, 419 U.S. 1096 (1974).

for the Fifth Circuit, however, held Wyeth liable, finding the prescription drug rule inapplicable, since the immunization setting was effectively a mass immunization program.

This theory of liability has since been expanded to include immunizations provided by private physicians. In *Givens* v. *Lederle*,[34] an unimmunized mother contracted polio after her daughter had been vaccinated with oral polio vaccine by a private pediatrician. The Fifth Circuit affirmed a verdict against Lederle for failure to take steps to warn the mother directly. The pediatrician's office procedures were found sufficiently analogous to those employed in a public clinic, as in *Reyes,* to warrant a direct warning to the consumer. Consequently, a manufacturer who seeks protection against liability has come to assume that its vaccines will be used without individualized medical attention. Thus the manufacturer attempts to ensure that a warning reaches each potential consumer.

The vaccine cases have presumed that had parents received a warning of vaccine risks, they would have acted to minimize the risks and refused immunization, thereby escaping injury. This presumption parallels that applied to informed consent cases and establishes that the failure to warn is the proximate cause of the injury. Only in *Cunningham* v. *Charles Pfizer & Co.*[35] was an objective test permitted to overcome the presumption. There, the Oklahoma Supreme Court found that the existence of an epidemic might have induced a reasonably prudent person to accept vaccination even if properly warned against the risks of the vaccine.

Vaccine manufacturers have expressed concern over the potential liability they face under the vaccine case principles, largely because they cannot ensure that consumers receive the required warnings. Most have entered into contracts that require the public health authorities that purchase vaccines to issue the warnings to consumers. The effect of such contracts remains somewhat unclear. The doctrine of sovereign immunity protects state and federal governments against suits for personal injury, leaving manufacturers as potential defendants despite their efforts. Under the swine flu program,[36] federal legislation was required to permit the federal government to assume the duty to warn and agree to be sued for nonnegligent injuries attributable to the vaccine.

Although physicians could be held responsible for vaccine

34. 556 F.2d 1341 (5th Cir. 1977).

35. 532 P.2d 1377 (Okla. 1974).

36. National swine flu immunization program of 1976, 90 Stat. 1113, 42 U.S.C. sec. 247b(j)-1 (1976).

related injuries in which they have negligently administered a vaccine or failed to disclose its risks to the recipient, physicians have rarely been the target of such lawsuits. The doctrine of informed consent requires physicians to advise patients of the possible risks of treatment.[37] In most states, the scope of disclosure—what must be disclosed to the patient—is measured by the prevailing practice of physicians in the community. The more recent trend, followed in a minority of states, measures the scope of disclosure by what is "material" to the patient's decision.[38]

The manufacturer's duty to warn and the doctrine of informed consent are both premised on the notion that a vaccine recipient is free to decide whether or not to undergo vaccination. The right to decide is protected by the receipt of information about vaccine risks and benefits, which can be weighed by the patient in light of his or her own circumstances. However, not all immunization decisions are voluntary. State laws often require children to be immunized against certain diseases as a condition of entering school. Military personnel are obliged to undergo certain vaccinations. And many people accept vaccines in mass immunization programs at the urging of public health authorities. The use of tort law concepts of the duty to warn and of informed consent to allocate liability for injury in such cases may be considered unfair, because a person who has received an adequate warning is precluded from recovering any compensation for a resulting adverse reaction, even if he could not lawfully refuse the vaccine.

Costs and benefits of reliance on tort law

Tort law, which assigns financial responsibility for drug and vaccine related injuries and provides compensation to those injured, requires the injured party to bring a claim against the responsible party. Litigation thus enforces rights and responsibilities recognized by law. Of course, not all injuries result in claims, and not all claims result in lawsuits. To assess whether tort law is an adequate mechanism of enforcement and whether it achieves its goals at a reasonable cost, it is useful to examine the costs of litigation. Unfortunately, data on the costs of drug and vaccine litigation are scarce. The following categorization of the types of costs of drug and vaccine litigation is a first step on the way to determining costs to defendants, plaintiffs, and society at large.

37. Arnold J. Rosoff, *Informed Consent: A Guide for Health Care Providers* (Rockville, Md.: Aspen Systems Corporation, 1981).

38. *Canterbury* v. *Spence*, 464 F.2d 772 (D.C. Cir. 1972); *Cobbs* v. *Grant*, 8 Cal. 3d 229, 104 Cal. Rptr. 505, 502 P.2d 1 (1972).

Costs of Defending Claims

The costs to a pharmaceutical company of defending product liability litigation fall into three categories.

Direct expenses of litigation. This category includes attorneys' fees paid to outside counsel (defense lawyers who are not employed by the defendant), expert witness fees, court costs, stenographic expenses of depositions and trials, travel expenses, and similar out-of-pocket expenses paid to defend a particular claim or lawsuit.

Indirect expenses of litigation. This category includes costs that are not easily allocated to particular claims but arise largely in response to the threat or presence of litigation. The most salient cost is the expense of liability insurance, whether purchased from commerical insurers or reserved from a company's own assets. It includes a portion of the salaries of in-house counsel (attorneys employed by the defendant) and administrators, such as risk managers, claims adjusters, data processors, and insurance liaisons, charged with reviewing and evaluating potential claims, as well as nonsalary administrative expenses of claims review.

Here lies a number of the hidden costs of litigation—those that may be overlooked when focusing on compensation paid and attorneys' fees. For example, although most pharmaceutical companies engage outside counsel to conduct trials and serious settlement negotiations, they employ attorneys in-house to supervise the initial claims review and the work of outside counsel. The discovery process in litigation consumes a substantial (if, as yet, unquantified) proportion of in-house counsel's time to identify and review relevant documents (perhaps the entire new drug application file pertaining to the drug at issue), to translate medical opinion for purposes of determining proximate cause, and to evaluate the merits of claims made. Since most cases are won or lost on the issue of proximate cause, a substantial amount of time and money may be spent investigating the drug's properties and available research studies to determine whether the drug or some other factor could have precipitated an injury. Discovery may consume up to two years.

Claims review, which may involve claims adjusters, staff scientists and physicians, supervisors, and executives, may be a distinct administrative unit or part of a program of monitoring drug reactions. Nevertheless, to the (presumably large) extent that it is responding to claims of injury, it should be considered a cost of defense. Such expenses do not include payments made to claimants, but do include the cost of assessing claims and determining whether and how to defend.

General overhead expenses can be included in indirect expenses to the extent that they are directly attributable to claims review or to in-house counsel's efforts regarding litigation.

Also included are expenses occasionally incurred in allocating liability among those potentially responsible for payment—among defendant pharmaceutical companies, as in some DES cases, or between a defendant manufacturer and its insurers. These expenses include indirect costs of administration, as well as direct costs of conducting separate litigation, to determine who is responsible for paying what. They are included here because they are not part of the original litigation brought by the injured drug or vaccine recipient.

Finally, one might argue that the costs of providing a warning of drug risks constitute indirect expenses of litigation. To the extent that the warning forms part of the drug labeling requirements of the FDA, it might better be deemed an ordinary cost of production. Special warnings, however, could be developed to implement the principles of court decisions. Most courts appear to assume that the costs of providing a warning are nominal. For items with very low profit margins and a high volume of sales, even a few cents per dose could render the drug too uneconomical for a company to produce.

Compensation paid to injured claimant. This, the most obvious of costs, includes all payments to claimants. Payments may occur because of a judgment after trial or because of the voluntary settlement of a claim before, during, or after trial. It is the gross amount paid out to claimants, without any deduction for the claimants' own costs of litigation (such as their own attorneys' fees).

Although data concerning the number or amounts of claims made, settlements, or lawsuit outcomes in drug and vaccine litigation are rare, a few studies of other types of cases may suggest the size of costs in product liability litigation. The Rand study of asbestos litigation costs,[39] for example, found that defendant companies and their insurers incurred $661 million for closed claims as of August 1982. Of that total, $190 million (or 29 percent) constituted direct litigation expenses; $71 million (or 11 percent) were for indirect expenses; and $400 million (or 60 percent) were paid in compensation to claimants. Whether these figures are comparable, even in relative magnitude, to those incurred in the defense of drug or vaccine claims is an open

39. James S. Kakalik and others, *Costs of Asbestos Litigation* (Santa Monica, Calif.: Rand Corporation, 1983).

question, especially given the unique nature of asbestos litigation. The figures suggest that the amount of compensation paid to claimants does not represent the full costs of litigation.

The Rand study also found that of the approximately 3,800 claims that had been closed, about 18 percent were dismissed or withdrawn, 78 percent were settled before trial, and only 4 percent reached trial (some of which were later settled). The average payment by one such defendant to one plaintiff was approximately $3,000. But since several companies were defendants in one claim, the average total received by a plaintiff was considerably more, approximately $60,000. There is reason to believe that the amount of compensation awarded to a successful claimant as a result of a trial is substantially larger than that paid in settlement of a claim. The study estimated that the average payment in settlement was $64,000, while the average compensation paid for claims tried in court was $275,000.

The average amount paid by one defendant in direct litigation expenses to close an asbestos claim by one plaintiff was approximately $1,400. Because the claims involved multiple defendants, the average amount of such expenses per claim was $25,000, with settled or dismissed claims averaging $21,000, and claims going to trial averaging $116,000. Total defense costs, including direct and indirect expenses, were estimated to average $35,000 per closed claim. Interestingly, those defendants who paid higher compensation awards to claimants had a lower direct expense to compensation ratio than defendants who paid lower amounts in compensation. One explanation offered for this anomaly is the minimum level of threshold expenses (claims review and the like) incurred in defending any claim. Although expenses of litigation rise somewhat with increased compensation, the expenses rise less rapidly than the payments.

Direct litigation expenses as a percentage of compensation paid appear higher in asbestos cases than in cases of product liability and medical malpractice, although the ratio of 0.42 for asbestos cases is not much higher than the ratio of 0.35 for product liability cases. One reason that other types of cases may generate lower expenses as a proportion of compensation paid is that they typically involve only one defendant who pays the entire amount of compensation. The larger the award, the smaller the expenses as a percentage of compensation. The complexity of the asbestos cases may also contribute to higher expenses, although economies of scale may be achieved through the cooperation of multiple defendants. Some drug and vaccine litigation involves fairly complex issues of causation and may require extensive, expensive discovery. It may be that the DES cases are more comparable to asbestos litigation than are individual cases for drug related injury.

A recent Rand study of jury verdicts and awards in civil trials over the past twenty years in San Francisco and in Cook County, Illinois, concluded that awards were strikingly similar in the two jurisdictions.[40] The authors compared the results of verdicts in suits for money damages involving product liability, professional malpractice, contracts and business torts, intentional torts, injury to workers, street hazards, property liability, and automobile accidents and common carriers' liability for passenger injury. They found that in the latter part of the 1970s the number of lawsuits filed increased, but the number of jury trials dropped. At the same time, trials involving product liability, malpractice, intentional torts, and contract and business torts increased sharply, occupying about a third of civil jury trials by the late 1970s. Some of this increase, as a percentage of all civil jury trials, may be explained because such cases involved serious injuries and complicated issues. The amount of damages claimed was higher, raising the stakes sufficiently to warrant a trial.

The same study found that plaintiffs now succeed in malpractice trials in about one out of three cases. In product liability cases, 40 percent of plaintiffs won jury verdicts in Cook County, and 54 percent won in San Francisco. The impact of the growing success of plaintiffs is influenced strongly by how much they recover at trial.

The size of jury awards appears to be moving in two directions at once. Most recoveries remained about the same over the years preceding 1980, increasing slightly before 1975 and declining thereafter. A recent few blockbuster cases, however, achieved awards at or near $1 million. A small percentage of cases (between 1.2 percent and 2.3 percent) accounted for 40 to 50 percent of the total amount of all jury awards. These few large awards raise the reported average dollar amount of verdicts (over 300 percent for product liability and over 500 percent for malpractice), but do not benefit most plaintiffs, whose awards have not increased. For example, during the 1970s the median (typical) recovery in a malpractice action decreased steadily in San Francisco, yet the average increased. One case alone—with a $6.6 million judgment—represented 60 percent of all malpractice awards in San Francisco

40. Michael G. Shanley and Mark A. Peterson, *Comparative Justice: Civil Jury Verdicts in San Francisco and Cook Counties, 1959–1980* (Santa Monica, Calif.: Rand Corporation, 1983).

in the early 1970s. Because of such large awards, malpractice and liability cases now account for a higher proportion of all dollars awarded to plaintiffs in civil trials than they did in the 1960s.

Publicity surrounding large verdicts tends to heighten concerns that litigation is too costly a mechanism for resolving disputes. The reduced number of smaller claims tried and their decreasing recoveries point to a similar, often overlooked, problem: the monetary stakes in small cases are often less than the costs of litigation to the parties. A small number of complex claims for large amounts are consuming more and more court time, as well as producing the bulk of the awards to plaintiffs, suggesting that litigation is becoming less effective in addressing simple problems with low financial values.

Over a decade ago, Professor Robert Keeton estimated that victims of automobile accidents received about forty-four cents out of every dollar of automobile accident insurance, with the balance being spent on claims administration and overhead:[41]

Distribution of $1.00 of Automobile Insurance for Liability for Bodily Injury

General overhead		33.0¢	
Claims administration cost			
Defense side	13.0¢		
Claimants' side	10.0¢		
Total claims administration cost		23.0¢	
Total overhead			56.0¢
Net amount paid to victims above losses (in theory for pain and suffering)	21.5¢		
Paid to compensate for losses also compensated from other sources (including some income tax saving)	8.0¢		
Paid to compensate for losses not compensated from other sources	14.5¢		
Net paid to victims altogether			44.0¢
			$1.00

In extrapolating similar figures for medical malpractice liability insurance premiums (seventy-two cents for total overhead; twenty-eight cents for victims), Professor Jeffrey O'Connell argued that the tort system fails to return adequate compensation to the victim while imposing unnecessary burdens on claimants, defendants, and insurers.[42]

41. Page Keeton and Robert E. Keeton, *Torts, Cases & Materials* (St. Paul, Minn.: West Publishing, 1977).

42. Jeffrey O'Connell, "An Alternative to Abandoning Tort Liability: Elective No-Fault Insurance for Many Kinds of Injuries," 60 *Minnesota Law Review* 501 (1976).

Costs of Bringing a Claim

Costs incurred by plaintiffs in pursuing product liability claims may be categorized as follows:

Direct expenses of litigation. Qualitatively comparable to the expenses incurred by defendants, the direct expenses of litigation include attorneys' fees, medical examinations, expert witness fees, court costs, deposition costs, loss of wages for time spent in court, travel, and other out-of-pocket expenses. For the most part, attorneys in such cases are paid on a contingency fee basis, receiving from 25 percent to 45 percent of the compensation, if any, received by the plaintiff.

The Rand asbestos litigation cost study estimated that direct expenses other than attorneys' fees were generally 6 percent to 9 percent of the compensation awarded in cases tried, and 5 percent to 6 percent in settled cases. Plaintiffs' attorneys will incur the foregoing types of costs without reimbursement if a case is handled on contingency and no award is made.

Indirect expenses of litigation. Indirect expenses incurred by plaintiffs differ from those incurred by defendants, since plaintiffs in drug and vaccine injury cases are usually individuals rather than organizations with claims processing units. These individuals may incur expenses that are not directly attributable to litigation (as are court costs, for example). Those expenses may result from the injury complained of, or they may contribute to the prosecution of the claim. Such expenses may include the plaintiff's own time spent in preparation for trial, lost income of family members who must care for the injured plaintiff, and medical expenses above and beyond those essential for treatment of the injury.

Economic losses. The losses suffered by a claimant as a result of taking a drug or vaccine constitute the damages sought in litigation. Although not properly an expense of litigation itself, such losses should be considered in any evaluation of litigation as a means of compensating injury. Such losses include income lost during periods of disability and unemployment; medical expenses incurred in the diagnosis and treatment of the injury, such as hospital charges, physicians' fees, nursing and rehabilitation expenses; and costs of medications and therapeutic devices.

Social Costs and Benefits

Besides directly affecting the parties to litigation, the use of tort law to allocate liability for and compensate injury related to drug and vaccine use generates costs and benefits to society at large. Since such social costs and benefits are often intangible, spread over large populations, and rarely directly ascertainable as resulting from litigation, they are difficult to identify and perhaps impossible to quantify. Yet use of tort law rather than some other means to resolve disputes in given types of cases certainly affects society. For example, the increasing amount of court time consumed by product liability and malpractice litigation delays or precludes the judicial resolution of other types of cases. A portion of the salaries of judges, clerks, stenographers, and court administrative personnel, as well as jurors' time, could be considered a social cost of litigation. Losses in employee productivity could be attributed to involvement in litigation.

The time and money spent by expert witnesses seems directly attributable to reliance on litigation. One study estimated that civil jury trials cost taxpayers between $3,000 and $15,000.[43] Various health care costs may also be incurred beyond those reasonably necessary to diagnose and treat injuries because of the need to establish or refute injury, damage, and causation solely for purposes of litigation. These may entail prolonged hospital stays, excessive tests and visits to physicians, unnecessary use of medications and devices, and the like. The threat of nonmeritorious litigation has also been cited by manufacturers as a potential reason for withdrawing certain drugs and vaccines from the market. Court decisions holding manufacturers responsible for injuries resulting from rare side effects or adverse reactions to drugs or vaccines may influence the stringency with which the FDA evaluates the safety and effectiveness of new drugs. Consequently, the licensing of potentially beneficial products may be delayed or prevented.

In the absence of detailed data concerning the costs and benefits of litigation, it is difficult to determine whether the tort law system is serving or defeating its goals. Sufficient uneasiness exists, however, to have produced frequent calls for reforming the system.[44] Changes intended to reform, rather than replace, tort

---

43. J. S. Kakalik and A. Robyn, *Costs of the Civil Justice System: Court Expenditures for Processing Tort Cases* (Santa Monica, Calif.: Rand Corporation, 1982).

44. Comment, "Immunization Injuries: Proposed Compensatory Mechanisms—An Analysis," 11 *Connecticut Law Review* 147 (1978); Comment, "Informed Consent to Immunization: The Risks and Benefits of Individual Autonomy," 65 *California Law Review* 1286 (1977); and Gerald Dworkin, "Compensation and Payments for Vaccine Damage, 1978–79," 1978–79 *Journal of Social Welfare Law* 331. H. J. Glasbeck and R. A. Hasson, "Fault—The Great Hoax," in Lewis Klar, ed., *Studies in Canadian Tort Law* (Toronto: Buttersworth, 1977), pp. 395–424; and Irving Ladimir, "Mass Immunizations: Legal Problems and a Proposed Solution," *Journal of Community Health*, vol. 2 (Spring 1977),

law are usually designed either to (a) increase the ability of injured persons to recover compensation, or (b) limit the liability of defendants. Few reforms within tort law can do both at once. For example, statutory changes tightening strict liability, expanding long-arm jurisdiction, eliminating requirements of privity, extending warning duties to include foreseeable misuse of products, broadening statutes of limitations to run from the date of discovery of injury, and the development of industrywide forms of liability are designed to ease the plaintiff's burden of proof. Such reforms are likely to increase the number of allowable claims and therefore the costs of litigation. Reforms benefiting defendants, such as allowing defenses based on the state of the art at the time the product was made, the use of a product beyond its reasonable life, and modification of a product after sale, are likely to inhibit plaintiffs' recoveries and may reduce claims and defendants' costs, while increasing the costs to plaintiffs who do sue. These defense proposals, however, are not likely to apply to many drug or vaccine cases.

Alternatives to the tort law system have unknown costs and benefits. Proposals for an administrative mechanism to replace litigation have most often concerned vaccine injury. In 1983 Senator Paula Hawkins introduced a bill to create a federal national vaccine injury compensation program.[45] It is unclear whether that proposal can solve the problems it is intended to address without generating excessive costs. The swine flu program, which few would cite as an example to be followed to the letter, received 4,152 claims for injuries allegedly resulting from swine flu immunizations totaling more than $3 billion as of the end of 1983. Amounts paid by the federal government to settle claims equaled $39,866,344, and payments made upon judgments were $33,088,941. Although this represents an average of less than $2.00 per claim, the cost of administering such claims is not yet known.

Tort liability for personal injury is intended to act as a quality control device, providing a clear incentive to produce safe and

---

pp. 189–208; William K. McIntosh, "Liability and Compensation Aspects of Immunization Injury: A Call for Reform," 18 *Osgood Hall Law Journal* 584 (1984); National Immunization and Work Group on Liability, "Report and Recommendations," in *Reports and Recommendations of the National Immunization Work Groups* (Department of Health, Education, and Welfare, 1977); U.S. Congress, Office of Technology Assessment, *Compensation for Vaccine-related Injuries* (GPO, 1980); and U.S. Department of Health, Education, and Welfare, *Liability Arising Out of Immunization Programs: Final Report to Congress* (GPO, 1978).

45. National Childhood Vaccine Injury Compensation Act, S. 2117, 98 Cong. 1 sess. (GPO, 1983).

effective products and deterring dangerous practices and outcomes. It may be an inefficient and often inequitable means of ensuring quality, but it is all that is available. If tort law is to be replaced, it is fair to ask whether the replacement can ensure quality at least as well. To that question, there are no clear answers. Professor Patrick Atiyah has noted that the level of workers' compensation benefits available has no obvious correlation with the frequency of industrial accidents. He reviewed the study by the National Commission on State Workmen's Compensation Laws, which found that several states with similar benefit levels had widely different accident levels, while other states with similar accident levels had very different benefit levels.[46]

In medical malpractice, the desire to achieve quality has been linked to counterproductive outcomes, with some physicians ordering unnecessary, occasionally risky, tests and procedures in the practice of defensive medicine. Although there is little evidence of the prevalence or cost of such practices and even less of the assertion that they harm patients,[47] the widespread perception that malpractice law spawns inappropriate and costly practices remains. One might wonder whether product liability law fosters defensive manufacturing, that is, the taking of unwarranted measures as a prophylaxis against product liability claims. Indeed, given the absence of judgment as an element in defining sound manufacturing practices (as opposed to medical practice), the potential for introducing unnecessary and counterproductive procedures in producing drugs and vaccines seems quite low. Manufacturers who spend more to test and ensure the safety and efficacy of their products are not subjecting the public to a greater risk of harm, except, possibly, that of delaying distribution of a beneficial product. But product liability is not the only quality control mechanism applied to the production of drugs and vaccines. The licensing requirements of the FDA provide a far more direct, although not infallible, means of promoting safety and efficacy than the less predictable threat of liability for personal injury. It is questionable whether FDA regulations would remain as strict as they are if product liability law ceased to apply to drugs and vaccines.

---

46. Patrick S. Atiyah, *Accidents, Compensation, and the Law,* 3d ed. (London: Weidenfeld and Nicolson, 1975), pp. 606–07.

47. P. Munch Danzon, *The Frequency and Severity of Medical Malpractice Claims* (Santa Monica, Calif.: Rand Corporation, 1982).

A comparison of drug and vaccine litigation

The earlier review of theories of liability for personal injury reveals an essential identity of causes of action whether the product at issue is a drug or a vaccine. Similarly, litigation costs to plaintiffs and defendants are the same basic type for both drug and vaccine cases. Yet the implications of litigation concerning each of the two classes of products are not necessarily the same.

A claimant who believes he was injured as the result of taking either a drug or a vaccine may seek compensation for his injury from the manufacturer. The claimant must establish that the manufacturer who produced the product was negligent either in manufacturing or in distributing the product, thereby rendering it defective, or failed to issue a warning of the risks inherent in a pure and properly manufactured product. Given the sophistication of current manufacturing and quality control procedures, the production of an impure or tainted drug or vaccine is rare. Accordingly, the more likely cause of action for drug or vaccine litigation is based on the manufacturer's duty to warn.

The incentive provided by tort law to manufacturers to produce safe products, whatever it may have been several decades ago, is probably negligible today. The regulatory requirements for testing pharmaceuticals and biologics as a condition of licensing have largely preempted the admonitions contained in case law to ensure the safety and effectiveness of such products. As a result, the duty to warn serves only to ensure that information about risk reaches the proper party to enable him or her to decide whether a particular drug or vaccine is appropriate. The duty is not likely to increase the manufacturer's own knowledge of the risks of its products, since premarket testing will have revealed most adverse reactions. Where risks could not have been discovered at the time of production, given the state of science at that time, the duty to warn cannot force manufacturers to do the impossible. Subjecting manufacturers to strict liability in such cases might encourage careful testing, but it is not likely to produce a dramatic reduction in unknown risks. With respect to products falling within the prescription drug rule, in cases where warnings are directed to physicians via package circulars, the duty to warn does not appear to impose a new or additional burden upon manufacturers. Similarly, the duty does not seem to create any independent, onerous obligation to disclose the risks of over-the-counter drugs in cases in which package inserts are otherwise required to acquaint the consumer with the risks of the drug.[48]

48. Of course, it is possible that the FDA could relax its regulations, leaving tort law a major force for promoting safety.

The expanded version of the duty to warn applied in the vaccine cases, however, does impose additional burdens upon manufacturers—to get a warning directly to the ultimate recipient of a vaccine. Since manufacturers cannot be present in a physician's office or clinic when vaccines are administered, they must rely on third parties, such as physicians or local public health authorities, to distribute risk information to consumers. If no warning is issued, the manufacturer faces the prospect of liability for injuries resulting from an undisclosed risk, whether or not the party administering the vaccine may also be responsible. Yet the manufacturer is not in a position to guarantee that the proper warning is given and thus avoid liability.

This aspect of product liability for vaccine injury has provoked serious concern by vaccine manufacturers. They complain of being subject to unpredictable financial responsibility for incidents that they cannot control. Although the incidence of adverse reactions is almost equally predictable (or unpredictable) for drugs and vaccines, the probability of liability for adverse reactions to vaccines depends upon the presence or absence of warnings that the manufacturer does not directly provide. The increasing willingness of individuals to sue to recover compensation for personal injuries compounds the problem. A few television programs and newspaper articles highlighting serious injuries, usually those suffered by children, have heightened public awareness of the potential risks of immunizations. Public health officials fear that focusing on the risks, rather than the benefits, of vaccines will lead to a dangerous decline in the public's acceptance of immunizations, with serious consequences for the prevention of disease and death.

Public perceptions of the risks of immunizations thus affect both the production of vaccines and the public health. Faced with an unknown potential liability to a population that is increasingly intolerant of risks to health and increasingly willing to sue, many vaccine manufacturers have stopped producing vaccines. Although most vaccines remain available in this country, many, such as those for polio and measles, are now produced by only one company. Whether these monomanufacturers will continue to supply such important commodities for disease prevention is a major public policy concern. The economics of vaccine production and distribution are not encouraging. Profit margins on vaccines are low, and manufacturers are reluctant to raise prices to cover their liability exposure, partly because they are unsure of the amount of such exposure, and partly because they recognize that increased vaccine prices may deter the purchase and administration of needed vaccines.

Manufacturers also argue that patent protection is more limited for biologics than for most pharmaceuticals, leaving producers with a relatively smaller return on their investment. The reluctance of the insurance industry to provide specific liability insurance coverage for claims related to vaccines is significant. This leaves many vaccine manufacturers as self-insurers of their liability for vaccine related claims. Under these circumstances, there is little incentive for pharmaceutical houses to produce existing vaccines or to spend the considerable time and money necessary to develop new vaccines.

Despite the effectiveness of most vaccines in preventing disease, physicians often have little incentive to offer immunizations. Their education rarely includes training in the efficacy of immunizations; it is often difficult to recommend that well patients subject themselves to even the minute risks of a vaccine; and health insurance does not cover such preventive measures.

The liability issue exacerbates the unfavorable economic climate for the production and distribution of vaccines. The law governing vaccine injury does not always fit the reality of immunization practices. Immunization is often a public good; its benefits extend beyond the individual vaccine recipient to the public at large. For many diseases, if enough people are vaccinated, herd immunity operates to protect even the unvaccinated. In other cases, as with live virus vaccines, person-to-person spread of the attenuated vaccine virus provides secondary protection of unvaccinated members of the community. The benefits of vaccines to the public health have long induced both federal and state governments to promote immunizations. Government is involved in immunization programs to a far greater degree than it is in other health services, from testing and licensing the vaccines, to recommending immunization policy, to purchasing and administering vaccines. Yet despite the extensive involvement of government in immunization programs for the benefit of the public health, the law allocating liability for vaccine related injury continues to assume that immunizations are a private matter. Where liability and compensation are premised on the duty to warn, the law allows recovery only where there has been a failure to disclose risks, even in cases in which the vaccine recipient is not free to refuse the vaccine. The public nature of immunizations suggests that liability for vaccine injury should be assumed by the public, at least with respect to vaccines that are required, and perhaps those that are recommended, by public authorities.

In contrast, the use of pharmaceuticals is most often a private matter. Individual patients and physicians make voluntary decisions concerning the use of a drug. Then, the duty to warn can be justified as a means of allocating liability. It does not appear to add substantially greater costs to the production and development of pharmaceuticals. Assuming the value of allowing users of drugs to be aware of both a drug's positive and negative properties, the duty to warn may serve a proper social function at a relatively small marginal cost. Wholesale replacement of tort law applicable to such cases hardly seems necessary. And indeed, there has been no outcry among pharmaceutical companies that tort law needs to be replaced to solve their problems of liability for drug injury.

The foregoing suggests that differences in the function and use of drugs and vaccines may well warrant different mechanisms to deal with the occasional injuries that they may produce.

Conclusions

Reliance upon tort law to allocate liability for injuries related to drugs and vaccines and to compensate the injured appears to suffer from an inability to guarantee that only those responsible for injury pay the consequences, and all those suffering real injury receive equitable compensation. As litigation becomes more expensive, the inequities are magnified. The question that must be addressed is whether a disproportionate amount of health care expenditures is attributable to litigation. Although there are no precise data on the specific costs of litigation, it seems clear that litigation costs affect, probably negatively, the production and distribution of drugs and vaccines. Pharmaceutical houses do spend a substantial amount on processing and defending claims. Although the amounts devoted to litigation involving drugs may not be more than would be necessary under an alternative system, there is reason to believe that the costs of litigation involving vaccines may be as great or greater than the economic return that vaccines produce. Even if the costs are far lower than believed, the perception among producers, public health authorities, and the public that litigation threatens the future supply of pharmaceuticals and biologics may produce a self-fulfilling prophecy. To determine whether litigation is a counterproductive use of resources, research is needed to ascertain its true costs and their distribution throughout the population.

There is a caveat, however, when focusing on the costs of litigating personal injury claims. The high cost of litigation is cited as evidence of the need to reform the law. It is said that the present system undermines its own twin goals of limiting liability to those at fault and providing compensation to those actually injured. Proposed reforms are touted largely in proportion to their potential to achieve the goal of fair compensation. Yet reforms are not pursued unless they can reduce liability.

A fair compensation system could prove far more costly than litigation. After all, the number of injured persons who fail to seek redress through the law is not known. But, as Professor Jeffrey O'Connell points out, no one will listen to the reformer who says, "I can improve the system, but it will cost more."[49] Reforms become marketable when they claim to achieve the same objectives as the existing system—in a superior way at the same or lower cost. Therefore, reforms are being sold on the theory that they will cost less than the tort system.

In this manner, the cost of litigation insinuates itself into the debate as a ceiling on the cost of reform. Yet, as explained by Blum and Kalven, this condition distorts the debate.[50] For if reform is to provide fair compensation to the injured, without regard to the inequities and limitations of product liability, the amounts generated under product liability are irrelevant. Litigation recompenses only those who qualify under fault theories and who are able to press their claims successfully through the courts or gain settlements. The purpose of reforms, like no-fault compensation, is to eliminate those criteria for eligibility. But, if the total costs of litigation are viewed as the maximum pool of resources permitted under any reform, the result is merely to reshuffle the same resources among different claimants without regard to the new eligibility criteria. The reform's compensation pool is thus determined by the very system it was created to replace.

For this reason, it is wise to be cautious in using litigation costs as the sole justification for abandoning the tort law system. Admittedly, litigation has unproductive costs, and there may be ways to reduce them. But, fundamentally, complaints about litigation costs have more to do with the somewhat arbitrary and unpredictable way that they are distributed than with their aggregate amount. True reform must be directed at allocating liability to those who should be responsible for injury and securing compensation for those who are truly injured. Eliminating windfall gains and eliminating uncompensated losses are steps toward a more equitable system. Whether those reforms will reduce costs is a separate question.

49. Jeffrey O'Connell, "An Alternative to Abandoning Tort Liability."
50. Walter J. Blum and Harry Kalven, Jr., "Ceilings, Costs, and Compulsions in Auto Compensation Legislation," *Utah Law Review* 341 (1973).

Alternatives to the Present System of Litigation for Personal Injury

JOHN PRATHER BROWN

VIRTUALLY all commentators, with the likely exception of the personal injury plaintiffs' bar, agree that the present system of legal rules and procedures surrounding personal injury cases is in terrible shape. But there is no consensus about what its replacement should be. Doubtless, certain alternatives would significantly improve the present system. And also doubtless, certain changes could make the system worse.

This paper does not identify a best available system. Rather, it identifies the central issues raised by personal injury litigation and outlines the dimensions of the current problem. The paper also briefly describes some alternatives, a presentation better classified as a system designer's abbreviated handbook, rather than a pattern for legal revolution.

The legal responsibility for personal injury is at the center of an intricate web of issues. Crafting a wise alternative to the present legal system will require care, consideration, and meticulous attention to detail. The issues raised by the tort system and by the impact of possible changes are not just legal issues, and they are not just lawyers' issues. They are broad in effect and raise important political, philosophical, and economic questions. The more carefully that a broad range of people considers such questions, the more likely it is that changes will be wisely crafted.

The legal system and incentives for precautions

The most important effect of a change in liability rules is its potential impact on safety precautions taken by producers and suppliers. Changes in legal rules can lead to more accidents or fewer accidents. They can also affect production costs, so that goods and services can become more or less costly. Unfortunately, the causal link between legal change and production change is long, indirect, diffuse, and difficult to study. Still, this is the largest potential effect of any possible alternative, and it must be thoroughly explored. It behooves advocates to show that their systems will not harm incentives for proper precautions. For example, advocates of New Zealand style abolition of the tort system should explain how incentives for precautions will work. Advocates of strict liability should explain how they expect incentives for buyers' precautions to work.

Tort and product liability sanctions do provide incentives for manufacturers and suppliers to take precautions on behalf of their customers. But other incentives also exist. If the incentives supplied by the legal system are but a small part of the overall set of incentives, then legal changes that may reduce incentives to take precautions are reasonable. But if the incentives provided through the workings of the legal system constitute the great bulk of incentives, then concerns about any dilution of incentives to take precautions should prevail.

What are the incentives for manufacturers to take precautions that will protect consumers from injury? I can distinguish three sources of incentives for manufacturers and sellers to invest in precautions: direct choice by consumers of safer products or services; indirect market effects on the firm's reputation; and the fear of legal consequences of potential litigation.

Consumers want safer products and can often distinguish between more and less safe products. All else being equal, customers choose a safer product. But often many relevant precautions are unobserved or unobservable to consumers. The design of a car's gas tank is not observable to a customer, even though the consequences of an inappropriately designed gas tank could become extremely important at some awful moment.

Even if consumers cannot directly observe the precautions taken by a manufacturer, that information could somehow be collected and reflected in a manufacturer's reputation. A manufacturer's failure to take precautions can disastrously affect that manufacturer, as illustrated by the recent melancholy history of Fiat automobiles in the United States. One recent model, a well-designed and attractive car, had an important flaw: it rusted quickly. When the model was first introduced, it sold well. However, as the cars started to rust, word spread, and the car sales fell. Eventually Fiat had to abandon the U.S. market. Had the company invested more in precautions against rust, it might still be active in the U.S. market.

Finally, the threat of litigation provides incentives for sellers to take precautions. The theory of effects on incentives has been much discussed in the law and economics literature.[1] Any sub-

1. For a formal discussion of the economics of common law rules, see Brown, "Toward an Economic Theory of Liability," 2 *Journal of Legal Studies* 323 (1973); for a more general but quite controversial discussion, see Richard Posner, *Economic Analysis of Law,* 2d ed. (Little, Brown, 1977).

stantive rule of law must provide both parties with the same incentives operating independently that they would have if they were operating together, bearing all the costs and benefits. It has been shown under very stylized circumstances that the ordinary common law rules of negligence, with or without contributory negligence, provide just such incentives. (Ordinary common law rules of negligence hold the parties to a standard of care of reasonableness under the circumstances.) Just how robust those conclusions are is still a matter of conjecture, since little empirical work has been done on the matter.

However, unquestionably, some incentives are provided, as shown by the following example. In recent years, doctors have often admitted to practicing defensive medicine, ordering more x-rays and diagnostic tests than necessary for the patient, in order to have better evidence of reasonable behavior in case of later litigation. Here the legal system seems to provide too much incentive for precaution. In fact, these extra x-rays and tests are potentially harmful, often carcinogenic. In principle, they are themselves torts. However, it is the nature of the legal rules of evidence and causation that it is inordinately difficult to prove the causal link between the test or x-ray and the cancer. Here the peculiarities of the rules protect the doctor and consequently change his or her behavior, illustrating my point that the design of legal rules has important effects on behavior in the marketplace.

The costs of operating the present system

The present system is expensive to operate. A recent widely quoted study by the Rand Corporation of the costs of asbestos litigation found that of each dollar spent by the asbestos companies on the litigation, only thirty-seven cents reached the victim.[2] The rest went to the attorneys on both sides and for the other costs of the legal system. I analyzed the results of an extensive survey undertaken by the Federal Trade Commission. I found that even in the simplest and most homely case of an uncontested rear end collision, virtually all attorneys surveyed would take the case on a contingent fee basis (usually for a one-third fee).[3] And this is an example in which there would be plenty of insurance and admission of liability! This kind of routine case could be handled by clerks in a few hours if the system were more competitive and less adversarial and legalistic.

2. James S. Kakalik and others, "Costs of Asbestos Litigation" (Los Angeles, Calif.: Rand Corporation, 1983).

3. John P. Brown, "Competition and Contingent Fees: The High Cost of Civil Justice" (Washington, D.C.: Chase, Brown, and Blaxall, 1983).

The scope of a proposed change

The scope of a rule is the set of accidents that the rule covers. The scope of a proposed change affects not only the potential cost of the change but also its efficiency. When the rewards to a party are different on different sides of a legal boundary, boundaries will be litigated. The greater the scope of the change, the more widespread the effect of any precedent that is litigated. If there is a wide variety of special laws, then many common questions will have to be relitigated for each of the special laws. But, for a general statute, a decision on causation in a ranching case can also apply to a boating case.

Funding sources

Accidents impose costs. Different systems of compensation do not reduce the costs of accidents; they shift them. Only indirectly, by affecting incentives for precautions, do systems affect the amount and total cost of accidents. In fact, some systems might have the effect of increasing accidents by reducing the incentives for precautions. Health, disability, property, and life insurance contribute to funding compensation for victims of certain accidents. Workers' compensation, liability insurance, judgments and settlements against defendants, medicare, medicaid, social security, black lung programs, and various government welfare programs help fund the costs of accidents. So, too, do private charities. Finally, some of the costs of accidents are borne by the victims; these costs are unfunded.

The interrelationship between tort law and workers' compensation is Byzantine. A major complaint against the present legal system is that it does not consider various sources of funding. The winning plaintiffs can be doubly compensated, or the prior source of funding might have to go through a legal proceeding to get all or part of its money back. One of the most complex parts of the Kasten bill, discussed next, is the part that defines the relationship between product liability and workers' compensation.

Compensation and courts, agencies, and markets

Courts, government agencies, and markets can play a role in the compensation of accident victims. Different programs rely in different ways on the three instruments. Both courts and agencies are expensive mechanisms for resolving disputes, though the costs of using them are borne differently. The parties involved largely bear the cost of litigation, while taxpayers and the parties involved bear the costs of agencies.

Determining the relative merits and efficiencies of courts and agencies to find out how best to assign tasks to them awaits a well-developed theory of judicial and lawyer behavior on the one hand and a well-developed theory of bureaucratic behavior on the other. Only some elements of these theories are currently available.

Clearly, courts handle awards for pain and suffering quite badly. A jury or a court has no standard against which to measure its judgments. Consequently, some of the major determinants of pain and suffering awards have nothing to do with pain and suffering, but rather with the sympathy that the jury feels for a victim. Race, class, physical attractiveness, manner of speaking, and other aspects unrelated to pain and suffering affect the jury. In such cases emotional and shock tactics are most successful and the size of the award is least predictable. Strong arguments can be made for eschewing litigation for pain and suffering. Awards could be calculated based on a standard table, in the same way that private insurance makes awards based on tables. Most European countries handle these cases by using a table or by flat denial of awards for pain and suffering.

Predictability of the award

One of the most important characteristics of a legal system is the predictability of its awards or judgments. If the award is completely predictable, then there is nothing to litigate. But, when the possible outcomes are extremely variable and subjective, as in payments for pain and suffering, then every incentive arises to fight, to litigate, and to invest heavily in litigation. With such uncertainty and variability in rewards, it pays both sides to invest in legal strategy and tactics. Legal strategy and tactics can change the distribution of possible outcomes for a given set of facts. Therefore the effectiveness of lawyers as strategists and tacticians becomes valuable. But this value comes about only because the underlying legal rules allow such variability and arbitrariness.

Legal reform in the area of personal injury should cause an increase in the predictability of outcomes. Now the personal injury plaintiffs' bar will object, saying that each individual is different, each injury is different, and the amount of pain and suffering is different in each case. The present system, they will point out, deals with each case individually. So far, their points are well taken and undeniable. The problem comes when they incorrectly conclude that the present system is less error prone than a schedule would be. It is not only conceivable, but likely, that the errors in the present system are larger than those inherent in a schedule.

Most of the pain and suffering in society is neither reviewed by courts nor compensated by courts. Only occasionally can one find a defendant to sue. Usually, pain and suffering are left to people to deal with on their own. Prudent people anticipate that accidents will happen and insure against them. They buy health insurance, disability insurance, and life insurance. If there were demand for it, one could even imagine pain and suffering insurance, which would pay for pain and suffering, above and beyond medical costs and lost wages, just as in personal injury lawsuits. Certainly such insurance is conceivable and, in a technical sense, insurable. But insurance against pain and suffering is not available.

The nonexistence of that possible market is revealing. It says that ordinary prudent people are not willing to pay the costs in their own money to finance payments for pain and suffering to themselves. It is not worth the cost.

Mechanisms for resolving disputes

Carrying this line of reasoning further leads to an evaluation of the adversary system as a cost-effective method of fact finding. If it were an effective method, it would be used outside the legal system. For example, in principle one could write a policy for any kind of insurance, such as health, disability, or life, that had as its payoff, when the insured event occurs, the amount awarded by a jury after listening to evidence presented by advocates for both sides according to federal rules of civil procedure. Nobody would voluntarily choose such a procedure, for the obvious reasons that it is extraordinarily expensive and introduces an enormous amount of uncertainty. This outcome is absurd, since the purpose of insurance is to reduce uncertainty, not increase it.

This state of affairs suggests that the standard common law civil procedure is not appropriate for all decisions. It is probably not appropriate for many of the decisions it is used to make. It is therefore no surprise that alternate mechanisms for resolving disputes receive a lot of attention. These mechanisms include, but are not limited to, mediation and arbitration. An alternate mechanism will often be more accurate, and perhaps less expensive, than ordinary civil procedure. Some difficulties arise, however. One is structuring an alternative so that it is in both parties' interest to choose that mechanism. Another difficulty is determining the selection of the most appropriate mechanism. Should a system make a certain mechanism mandatory? Mandatory can mean that (1) the state can choose the mechanism or (2) when a contract is written between two parties, the contract can mandate what mechanism must be used to resolve which dispute.

Alternatives

There are countless alternatives to the present liability system. Those mentioned here illustrate the scope of possible alternatives.

They have interesting possibilities. Furthermore, they are not mutually exclusive; they can be mixed and matched.

A quasi-no-fault plan

Congressman Henson Moore of Louisiana has expressed his intent to introduce a medical malpractice reform bill in March 1985, a bill that Professor Jeffrey O'Connell helped to design.[4] The bill is limited to medical malpractice claims, but the logic of the proposal is not so limited. The bill would allow a potential defendant to force a settlement of a tort claim by offering within sixty days to pay the victim's economic loss (lost wages; further medical and hospital costs; rehabilitation and nursing care; the cost of obtaining a housekeeper; and the cost of adapting the victim's house and car to the incapacity). If the offer were made within the time limit, the victim's ability to bring an action in tort would be superseded. Any amount that the victim would be entitled to receive from collateral sources would be netted out to reduce the obligation of the health care provider. The bill would also provide for reasonable expenses to obtain legal advice. The provider would be obliged to pay within thirty days of acceptance any losses already incurred, and to continue to pay as further losses are incurred. This bargain would not be allowed to supersede a tort action where (1) wrongful death action is brought as a result of the victim's death, (2) the malpractice is intentional, or (3) the economic injury is so small and the injury so grievous that payment of only the economic injury would shock the conscience of society.[5]

The benefits of this proposal are significant. The system's costs would be greatly reduced. Usually, there would be nothing to litigate; legal fees would probably be greatly reduced. The financial incentives against malpractice would still be in place; the amounts would be lower and the variance would be greatly reduced. The difficult conflict in a doctor's roles between that of adversary and that of health care provider would be greatly reduced, so that providers could afford to be generous and could quickly get on with their business. Frivolous suits could be avoided by the provider's refusing to tender an offer, in which case the plaintiff would have the full remedies and risks of present tort law. Insurance would be much more easily rated, without having to

4. Henson Moore and Jeffrey O'Connell, "Medicare and Malpractice: Quasi No-fault Reform," 44 *Louisiana Law Review* 1267 (1984). The proposal is numbered H.R. 5400.

5. In a similar vein, Professor Jeffrey O'Connell has drafted an insurance policy, in effect in forty-seven states, for serious high school athletic injuries, under the auspices of the National Federation of State High School Associations. The policy is to finance a pre-accident commitment to make a postaccident offer of net economic loss in exchange for giving up tort remedies.

finance the litigation lottery. Insurance companies would be asked to predict the frequency of claims, not the predilections and emotions of juries.

The victims of malpractice would receive compensation almost immediately; their bills would be paid. They would give up the dubious benefit of playing the litigation lottery, for very high stakes. They would avoid large attorneys' fees and the great delays involved in trials. The amount of money owed would be straight-forward to calculate, with relatively little variance.

A federal uniform product liability law

In March 1984, the Senate Commerce Committee marked up S. 44, Senator Robert W. Kasten's bill for a Uniform Product Liability Law (the Kasten bill). The Kasten bill would replace all tort law dealing with product liability with a federal statute, which would be adjudicated in the state courts. The bill has been through a number of drafts and revisions. It would retain strict liability for manufacturing defects—the mouse in the bottle or the crack in the axle—while using negligence as the standard in cases involving design defects or failure to provide warnings about products. The bill is the subject of thousands of pages of commentary, which would be impossible to summarize here. Although some commentators would deny it, the proposal is a modest one. It would provide more defenses for defendants than is the case now, and it would give uniformity to the product liability law, which ought to reduce costs of legal advice. It would clearly return to a negligence standard in design and warning cases, situations where the alternative, strict liability, is difficult to interpret sensibly.

Marketability of claims

One of the more intriguing possibilities for reform is to make causes of action (legal claims) marketable by plaintiffs. This is a simple change, but one with a potentially profound impact. The idea is deregulatory in nature; it extends the scope of market exchange.

When an accident occurs, two things occur. The victim is hurt, and a contingent legal claim against a defendant is created. That contingent claim is an asset, just as many other contingent claims like lottery tickets, or insurance policies, or mineral rights in Oklahoma are assets. One distinctive characteristic of contingent claims against a defendant is that the claim cannot be sold, except to the defendant (a settlement).

Like other contingent claims, these are quite risky. On one hand, they are not appropriate assets to be held by many people, especially the poor. On the other hand, if they are collected, the law of large numbers applies and in a large portfolio of similar but independent contingent claims, the total risk is reduced.

And, like some other contingent claims, such as mineral rights, these assets are difficult to manage for most people who are unaccustomed to their management. For these reasons, there would be potentially great benefit to all parties if there could be an organized market in causes of action. Plaintiffs could exchange these risky, difficult to manage, complicated assets for immediate cash if they wished. Buyers could profit by pooling risks and by efficiently managing the claim. In particular, it is unlikely that professional managers of tort claim portfolios would hire lawyers (on a contingent-fee basis) and pay them a third of the claim. Defendants could of course enter the market for the claim, and if the price were right, extinguish the claim. Even if defendants did not buy the claim, they would be informed by the market value of the claim. The claim would tend to be transferred to the best manager, who could combine high-quality legal advice with lower costs.

But the sale of tort causes of action would be a violation of the ancient common law criminal causes of action, champerty and maintenance, and it is considered unethical for a lawyer to participate in such a sale. Why such sales were historically deemed crimes is unknown. The purpose of this ethical restriction is also unknown. Nonetheless, champerty and maintenance are still violations of lawyers' codes of ethics. Even if these barriers were swept away, another institution would have to develop. That is the legal analog of the certified public accountant, whose task would be to prepare a fair and reasonably accurate description of the claim so that potential bidders could easily and quickly evaluate it. A similar role is played by local banks, which prepare mortgages and standardize them so that they can be resold on the secondary market.

The New Zealand system

The New Zealand system deserves particular scrutiny because it is a clear and simple but radical alternative. In 1974 New Zealand abolished its common law tort system and its workers' compensation system and replaced them with a comprehensive, no–fault compensation scheme for accidents.

Anyone who suffers an accident is eligible for compensation from one of three public funds, one for those who earn income, one for those injured by automobiles, and one for those who do not fit into the first two categories. Those who suffer from diseases, other than occupational diseases, are not covered by the scheme. Levies on employers and on the self-employed, collected by the New Zealand counterpart to the Internal Revenue Service, fund the compensation for those who earn income. The rate for employers depends on the industrial activity of the employer, though there exists a possibility for varying rates for employers that have a better or worse than average accident rate for the particular industry.

The Post Office, in part of its motor vehicle licensing fee, collects funds for those injured by automobiles. General revenues supply the supplementary fund for those accidents that are not covered by the first two funds. The people usually covered by this fund are housewives, the retired, and visitors.

The benefits paid for by the system include the costs of medical care and earnings-related compensation, which is scheduled and goes up to 80 percent of a victim's earnings, to a maximum payment of $600 per week (as of 1981) while the victim is totally incapacitated. These payments are subject to income taxes, which are withheld. Benefits also include lump sums for permanent disability; rehabilitation services; and other expenses and losses from the injury, such as household services and damages to clothing. When the accident is fatal, the benefits include periodic and lump sum payments to surviving dependent spouse and children and funeral and other incidental expenses.

The definition of personal injury in New Zealand includes the physical and mental effects of injury or accident, iatrogenic injury ("medical misadventure" in the charming language of the statute), the results of occupational disease or industrial deafness, and bodily harm suffered because of any act or omission of any other person.

The results of heart attack or stroke, unless caused as a result of employment, and any damage to body or mind caused exclusively by disease, infection, or the aging process are not covered.

The administration of the system is handled by the local office of the Accident Compensation Commission, which has statutory responsibility for safety. Claims are made by filling out a simple form. Compared with the procedures necessary to assert a claim in a tort suit, this is childlike simplicity.

The New Zealand system cuts the link between the cause of the accident and compensation. It removes any incentive coming directly from the legal system for the manufacturer to take precautions. For this reason alone, the New Zealand experiment is fascinating. Theory suggests that the change in New Zealand law would significantly reduce incentives for precautions, causing more dangers and more accidents than would have occurred under the previous system. The new system has been in place ten years now. That is long enough to get some indication of how strong and how pervasive the effects on incentives are. Either possible result, that the legal change had had no effect on precautions or that it had large effects on precautions, would be important. A careful empirical study of the New Zealand experiment would probably benefit the United States' search for effective reform.

Conference Participants

Joel Ackerman
Jacob, Medinger, and Finnegan

Betty Jane Anderson
Associate General Counsel, American Medical Association

Grace Angst
Paluszek and Leslie

Jeffrey Axelrad
Director, Torts Branch, U.S. Department of Justice

Mary Ann Baily
Professor of Health Economics, The George Washington University

Robert Barnard
Senior Partner, Cleary, Gottlieb, Steen, and Hamilton

Mark Barrett
Senior Counsel, National Legal Center for the Public Interest

Elayne Bartner
Office of the General Counsel, U.S. Department of Energy

Walter E. Beach
Senior Staff Member, Center for Public Policy Education, The Brookings Institution

Frank Birows
Division Director, Environmental Protection Agency

Andrew Boesel
National Association of Schools of Public Affairs and Administration

Martin Boyle
General Attorney, Veterans' Administration

Cynthia Brown
Administrator, Washington Internal Medicine Group

John Prather Brown
Principal, Chase, Brown, and Blaxall, Inc.

Tom Brown
Policy Analyst, U.S. Department of Labor

Kathy Bryant
Legislative Counsel, American Medical Association

Paul Burdett
Director, Legislative Affairs, Merrell Dow Pharmaceuticals, Inc.

Edward J. Burger, Jr.
Director, Institute for Health Policy Analysis, Georgetown University Medical Center

81

Deborah J. Chollet
Research Associate, Employee Benefit Research Institute

Warren I. Cikins
Senior Staff Member, Center for Public Policy Education, The Brookings Institution

Paul Colborn
Senior Counsel, Office of Legal Policy, U.S. Department of Justice

Robert Copeland
Director, Office of Health and Disability, U.S. Department of Labor

C. Richard Cornelius
General Counsel, Children's Hospital, Washington, D.C.

Madeleine Crohn
President, National Institute for Dispute Resolution

John Cutrone
Staffing, Labor, and Employee Relations Division, Defense Logistics Agency

Patricia M. Danzon
Professor, Duke University

Kurt Darr
Professor, The George Washington University

Juan del Real
General Counsel, U.S. Department of Health and Human Services

William Donaldson
Merrell Dow Pharmaceuticals, Inc.

John Doyle
Staff Director, Senate Human Resources Subcommittee on the Handicapped

Phoebe Eliopoulos
Bureau of National Affairs

Charles Epps
Chairman of the Board, National Capital Underwriters, Inc.

Jeffrey Finn
American Hospital Association

Michael Freedman
Associate Director, Issue Development, Common Cause

Willis Goldbeck
President, Washington Business Group on Health

Delphis Goldberg
Consultant, Intergovernmental Relations

David Greenberg
Legislative Director, Consumer Federation of America

Stephen Halpert
Legal Counsel and Senior Staff Economist, Council of Economic Advisers

Susan Harris
Director of Legal Affairs, American Health Care Association

Ann T. Hunsaker
Assistant General Counsel, Health Care Financing Administration, U.S. Department of Health

Robert Ingram
Merrell Dow Pharmaceuticals, Inc.

Alice Jackson
National Association of Community Health Centers

Robert Jarman
Insurance and Claims Officer, Central Intelligence Agency

William Johnson
Professor, Syracuse University

Gwendolyn Jones
Employee Relations Specialist, Equal Employment Opportunity Commission

Laura Kalick
Tax Manager, Laventhol and Horwath

Robert Katzmann
Research Associate, Governmental Studies, The Brookings Institution

Cynthia King
Policy Analyst, Office of Technology Assessment

James Lambrinos
Professor, Union College

Mary Legatski
Manager, Regulatory Affairs, FMC Corporation

David Little
Chief Executive Officer, National Capital Reciprocal Insurance Company

William Lubeley
Vice-President, Mutual of Omaha

Miriam MacDonald
Washington Representative, Metropolitan Insurance Companies

Bruce K. MacLaury
President, The Brookings Institution

Wendy K. Mariner
Assistant Professor of Health Law, Harvard School of Public Health

Donna Marsh
Conference Assistant, Center for Public Policy Education, The Brookings Institution

Jacqueline Mazza
Research Assistant, Center for Public Policy Education, The Brookings Institution

Randolph Moore
Government Liaison, American Academy of Pediatrics

John Murphy
General Counsel, Veterans' Administration

Bernard Nelson
Executive Vice-President, The Henry J. Kaiser Family Foundation

Stuart Nightingale
Associate Commissioner for Health Affairs, Food and Drug Administration

Barry Oertel
Executive Personnel Division, Federal Emergency Management Agency

Jerry Olszewski
Paluszek and Leslie

Joseph Onek
Partner, Onek, Klein, and Farr

Alexander Orfinger
Research Assistant, Center for Public Policy Education, The Brookings Institution

Joseph Page
Professor of Law, Georgetown University

Frederick Panciera
Second Vice-President, Travelers Insurance Company

John E. Porter
U.S. Representative, Tenth District of Illinois

John Post
Resident Consultant, Center for Public Policy Education, The Brookings Institution

Meryle Price
Price Strategic Marketing

Francis Robicsek
Charlotte Memorial Hospital and Medical Center

William T. Robinson
Vice-President, American Hospital Association

John Rother
U.S. Senate Committee on Aging

Raymond Scalettar
Chairman, Professional Liability Committee, American Medical Association

Guenter Schindler
Economic and Tax Consultant, Schindler Associates

Alfred Schretter
Senior Staff Counsel, Merrell Dow Pharmaceuticals, Inc.

Victor Schwartz
Partner, Crowell and Moring

David Seitzman
Treasurer, Medical Society of D.C.

David Sharrock
Merrell Dow Pharmaceuticals, Inc.

Helen Lessin Shaw
Office of Legal Policy, U.S. Department of Justice

Jim Singer
Pharmaceutical Manufacturers Association

Fred Siskind
Labor Economist, U.S. Department of Labor

Edmond Smith
Account Executive, Hill and Knowlton

Dorothy Starr
National Capital Underwriters, Inc.

Anthony Steinmeyer
Appellate Staff, Civil Division, U.S. Department of Justice

C. Joseph Stetler
Partner, Dickstein, Shapiro, and Morin

Geraldine Stroud
General Counsel, Group Health Association

Harry Swegle
Washington Liaison, National Center for State Courts

Peter Szanton
Consultant, Endispute Inc.

Josiah Thomas
Office of Civilian Personnel, National Security Agency

Robert Thomas
Executive Director, National Association of Private Psychiatric Hospitals

Daniel Toomey
Wickwire, Gavin, and Gibbs

Ann Van Leer
Appropriations Associate, Office of Representative John E. Porter

Nila Vehar
The Conference Board

John Virts
Corporate Staff Economist, Eli Lilly and Company

Doug Walgren
U.S. Representative, Fifteenth District of Pennsylvania

Clark Watts
Chairman, Department of Neurosurgery, University of Missouri

Ruth Ann Weidel
Counsel, Special Senate Committee on Aging

Hans Weill
*Science and Public Policy Fellow, The Brookings Institution,
Doctor of Medicine, Tulane Medical School*

Russell Wheeler
Federal Judicial Center

Robert Willmore
Assistant General Counsel, Office of Management and Budget

Rhea Wilson
Sacramento Bee

Charles Wise
Acting Director, Intergovernmental Affairs, U.S. Department of Justice

Stanley Wisniewski
Connerton and Bernstein